What

"*Jim Karol is the most Amazing Mentalist on the planet and his extraordinary memory and mental abilities are Beyond Belief.*"

George Noory, National Talk Show Host
Coast to Coast AM

"*Jim Karol always captivates the cadets with his unique abilities. He is the Babe Ruth of MEMORY.*"

Ron Harsh, Cadet Activities
United States Military Academy
West Point, NY

"*Jim is a phenomenal and innovative entertainer. I've always been impressed with his energy, his passion and his unique style of entertainment. That is why we bring Jim back year after year.*"

Tim Butler, Director of Student Activities
Philadelphia University

"*I have shared in the joy of Jim's success as his legend continues to grow. His visits to SUNY Delhi are among our most popular events, filling the theater every year. Jim is the BEST of the BEST.*"

Marty Greenfield, Director of Student Activities
State University of New York
Delhi, NY

"Jim Karol has been providing cognitive memory programs at the USO Warrior Family Centers in Bethesda and Fort Belvoir. It has been incredible to see the changes in the service members and Wounded Warriors as they go through Jim's sessions, and to watch how Jim magically connects with them. Jim Karol takes brain wellness to a whole new level."

Elaine Rogers
President and CEO
USO of Metropolitan Washington

"If Jim Karol's brain was a car, it would definitely be a Ferrari! Exciting, Fun, and Simply Amazing. Jim's feats are Jaw Dropping, and there is no better Mentalist Around. Do yourself a favor and enter the world of the INCREDIBLE with Jim Karol."

Tom Danheiser
Senior Producer
Coast to Coast AM

"Jim Karol had me at, 'listening to the music strengthens the brain.' Most music lovers feel that intuitively, but now the scientific evidence is clear. Music improves our creativity, fine motor and spatial reasoning skills, enhances our visual attention, and even helps us stay focused during physical exercise. Researchers call it musical Neuroscience, and it's just one of those areas of brain development and emotional intelligence that Jim touches on in his captivating new book,

Beyond Emotional Intelligence. Jim's book is a must-read for anyone who wants to better understand the power of the human brain to enhance our lives, physically, mentally and emotionally."

Terry Hummel
Former Publisher
Rolling Stone Magazine

"The memory feats Dale Ledbetter can now do after training with Jim Karol are truly mind boggling."

Dr. Robert Willix, Founder
Enlightened Living Medicine
And Author of Age Proofing

"Jim Karol's ability to read a person's character and uncanny skill at quickly ascertaining if a person is being deceptive, are extremely unique and valuable."

Allen McCormick
Lt. Col. Psychological Operations
U.S. Army

"Your interactions with the Wounded Warriors and their families opened my eyes to how beneficial your kind of performance can be, especially, for those struggling with TBI and PTSD! You opened my MIND as well!!"

John McDonald
VP Corporate Communications and Public Affairs
American Airlines

"Jim Karol isn't just a memory and emotional intelligence expert. He skillfully shows attendees how they can maximize their own mental abilities."

Dr. James Hardt, Ph.D
Physics and Psychology, Biocybernaut Institute

"Jim Karol NEVER FAILS to entertain both young and old."

Fred Deluca
Founder of Subway

"Jim Karol possesses a remarkable ability and charisma and motivates and inspires people to follow their dreams."

Mat Franco
Winner of America's Got Talent

"I am riveted, mystified, and constantly amazed by Jim's seemingly 'out of body' ability to be able to accomplish what seems to be impossible. Jim has been an inspiration to our veterans, the medical profession and all who encounter him, not only by his miraculous feats, but by his constant giving of himself. He is beautiful, honest and a patriotic American, and I am proud to say, he is my friend."

Tony Lo Bianco
Actor, Director, Writer, Producer

"Jim Karol is not ONE in a million, he's not ONE in a billion, JIM is ONE ON THE PLANET."

Dr. Gene Neytman
Geriatrician/Internal Medicine

"I can't even imagine having our event without bringing in Jim Karol as our key note speaker. Jim's passion and energy bring out the best in everyone. Our scientists think he is superhuman."

Judy Muoio
Senior Event Planner
Products and Chemicals, Inc.

Beyond
Emotional
Intelligence

OTHER BOOKS BY JIM KAROL

Psychic Madman

50 Ways to Hustle Your Friends

OTHER BOOKS BY DALE LEDBETTER

Bringing in the Business

From Mother With Love

The Ultimate Sales Professional

How Wall Street Rips You Off—
and what you can do to defend yourself

Success Yearbook

Record Setting Sales

Beyond Emotional Intelligence

Jim Karol

with Dale Ledbetter

Re-orders:

LEI Publishing
6748 NW 65th Terrace
Parkland, FL 33067
954.540.3642

ISBN: 978-1-4951-7618-0

Cover by Michelle Renee McElhannon

Printed in the United States of America

This book is dedicated to the firefighters who died or were injured trying to save others on September 11, 2001, and to the many Wounded Warriors who were maimed fighting for the freedoms we all cherish.

Contents

Foreword

Jim Karol is an extraordinary magician, a one-of-a-kind mentalist, a phenomenal memory expert and an extraordinary poker player, but he is much more than that.

Jim Karol is an especially caring humanitarian, a devoted husband and father, a mesmerizing entertainer and a medical marvel performing mind feats that have not been done by anyone else on the planet, but, without a doubt, he is more than that.

This book is about how Jim Karol has accomplished so much in his lifetime. It is about how he has developed an incredible memory and enhanced emotional intelligence, which has been the guiding force to Jim contributing so much to the world.

Jim also does an immense amount of work with the USO, helping in the rehabilitation efforts of our Wounded Warriors. He combines his memory skills, emotional intelligence and his love of magic, in helping troubled teens throughout the country.

This book doesn't just tell the Jim Karol story. It uses numerous lessons from various fields, including poker, one of Jim's favorites, as specific tools for learning and applying the power of enhanced emotional intelligence.

Whatever field you are in, Jim shows you how to master the SKILLS of emotional intelligence. He shares his secrets for building a workable EQ platform from which you can achieve monumental success.

The book takes one more gigantic step. It isn't just a recitation of Jim's success and the success of others who have drawn so much from the miraculous formula of emotional intelligence. It doesn't just tell the story of amazing feats of memory. This book takes the most important step of all. It reaches across boundaries and provides a roadmap for you to make EQ an important part of your life.

I can speak from personal experience in relating the impact Jim Karol has had on my life. As a long time and avid amateur magician, I was familiar with Jim Karol's performances and many of the illusions he had created and taught to others. I was excited to meet him and jumped at the chance to work with him. The experience of being exposed to him and having the chance to learn from him far exceeded my expectations.

I am living proof that we are NEVER too old to learn. In the past six months of working with Jim Karol I have amassed more information and gained more insight to the vast potential of my own brain than in the past several decades combined.

I have memorized decks of cards, the presidents, state capitals, more than 200 countries of the world, pages of texts and the list goes on and on. I have incorporated brain training into my daily routine and look forward to those sessions with all the enthusiasm imaginable. I'm learning more in my 70s than I've ever learned in my lifetime.

The whole process brings a continuous smile to my face. I haven't had this much fun in years!

Regardless of your profession, occupation, age or station in life, you will find the lessons that Jim Karol teaches and the stories that he shares, combine to create the ideal EQ roadmap to get you where you want to go.

I am honored that Jim Karol invited me to share the responsibility of delivering his story and the message of heightened emotional intelligence to the world.

Welcome to the fascinating world of EQ!

—Dale Ledbetter

Acknowledgements

I want to thank Dale Ledbetter for helping me write this book. Tony Dottino, founder of the USA Memory Championships, deserves my sincere gratitude for introducing me to Dale and to the Florida Hospital Neuroscience Department.

Heartfelt thanks go to Elaine Rogers, President of USO Metro and her incredible staff, for allowing me to work with some of our Wounded Warriors, the most inspirational group of Americans I have ever met.

Thank you to Montel Williams for introducing me to Walter Reed Medical Center and the dedicated members of the medical staff.

A very special thanks goes to both Dr. Neil Grunberg and Dr. James Hardt, two of the most brilliant minds on the planet. Speaking of brilliant minds, I would also like to thank my very dear friend Fred Deluca, co-founder of Subway for his inspiration and wonderful ideas.

A BIG thanks goes to the number one radio show in the world, Coast to Coast AM and good friends George Noory, Tom Danheiser and Lisa Lyon.

My Brain Wellness Institute Team, led by my great friends Kit Eldredge and Dr. Tim Pfister get my deepest gratitude.

I, also, want to recognize and thank all the incredible athletes I have met and worked with over the years, especially Ray Lewis and Shaq, both of whom are extremely inspiring individuals.

I am, also, deeply grateful to Michelle McElhannon for her hard work in typing the manuscript and designing the book cover.

Introduction

I'll NEVER forget when I met Jim Karol. It was during the 16th USA MEMORY CHAMPIONSHIP. I was talking with Dr M. Fotuhi, a neuroscientist from Johns Hopkins University, when Jim walked up and introduced himself to us. Jim took a deck of cards out of his pocket and asked us to shuffle them, then give him the deck of cards back when they were shuffled. He then told us that he would try to remember the order of the entire deck in less than 30 seconds! Of course, we looked at him with incredulous disbelief, since NO ONE had EVER MEMORIZED a deck of cards in less than 1 minute.

Believe it or not, after only 29 seconds, Jim recalled the ENTIRE deck of cards, and that began a relationship that has continued until today. Shortly after, Jim invited me and two members of the USA Memory Team to see him in action at Adelphi University where he was doing a 90 minute show for several hundred freshmen who were going to be attending their first year of college. The auditorium was packed with almost a thousand students. Everyone absolutely loved Jim's show, but what was even more amazing, was the rush of students AFTER the show, wanting to see MORE of his demonstrations of memory and magic! No one wanted to leave, and Jim was just as happy to show them more and more.

Why did I have such an interest in Jim and what he was doing? I wanted to know what MORE could he do with his remarkable memory skills. I wondered WHO, in the science of studying memory would be interested in what Jim was capable of doing?

And why was I so fascinated with Jim Karol?

I have been studying the science of the brain and the latest discoveries for more than 20 years, subscribing to John Hopkins, Cleveland Clinic, UCLA, Berkeley, Duke, and Massachusetts General monthly newsletters with a main focus on the recent secrets of the human brain and its UNLIMITED potential. Utilizing this research in my consulting practice and seeing the incredible results that people were able to create when realizing the only limit to their own thinking, WAS their own thinking.

And here comes Jim Karol, the ultimate subject, the HOLY GRAIL of what neuroscientists have been searching for and studying for more than 30 years.

I have been around the best memory athletes and have never seen ANYONE demonstrate the incredible capacity of the human brain like Jim Karol!

I invited Jim as my keynote speaker at the 17th USA MEMORY CHAMPIONSHIP where he demonstrated his amazing feats of MEMORY. People who attended the event are still talking about Jim. He gave out more than 300 tickets with information on each. The information included a 12 digit bar code number, a country and the capital, and a movie with the star performers. Each ticket had a seat number from 1 to 300, and as I was host, I got to select the number of the ticket that Jim would then have to recall all of the information on. Just think of the effort in doing something like this. 300 tickets each with their own unique 12 digit bar code, plus countries, their capitals and a movie. Hundreds of people throughout the day trying to stump Jim, yet he was right every time!

After the U.S. Memory championships, I invited Jim to meet the Assistant Vice President of Neuroscience at Florida Hospital and upon seeing his abilities she immediately agreed to host a Boot Camp for the Brain that was attended by more than 300 hospital employees. Jim and I were to be the key speakers, so I asked Jim if he could memorize information that was related to the human body, since this was for a hospital. Two hours later, he called me back and told me it was done. All 206 bones of the human body were committed to memory. At the boot camp we asked if anyone knew all of the bones in the human body and only two people were able to do so. We had a skeleton on stage and Jim took it apart bone by bone, naming each one.

Finally to answer the question, so what good is all of this memory stuff? And that was quickly answered as I was telling Jim about my granddaughter having broken her ankle falling off the ladder of a bunk bed. She had been to several doctors and she was still having problems walking after months of tests, therapy and doctor visits. Jim returns with a suggestion as to what bone to have her current doctor check to see if it was misplaced and sure enough, Bulls eye! My granddaughter was finally treated properly and able to walk again without pain and a limp.

I have hosted 18 Annual Memory Championships, and I CONTINUE to be amazed by Jim's skills and abilities. His memory is beyond belief even to me! Jim has moved on to studying the human brain in more detail, including the nervous system, mitochondria, neurons, neurotransmitters and emotional intelligence. He has come a very long way from when I asked him to learn the skeletal system just a few months ago!

Jim Karol continues to learn and prove what scientists are researching everyday….. the full capabilities of the HUMAN BRAIN, and Jim Karol is DEFINITELY their model to be studied!

Tony Dottino,

Founder, USA Memory Championships

Chapter 1

The Evolution of Jim Karol
From Steel Mill to Gold Mind

"Be the Change You Want to See in This World."
—*Gandhi*

I became a professional performer at the age of 29. Now, after more than 3500 shows, I have become a regular performer in the college and corporate markets. I have had the privilege of performing for, AND with, some of the biggest names in show business. I have gone from performing at comedy clubs to lecturing for hospitals and medical facilities.

I have evolved from someone who did a few magic tricks, into a more diversified performer, specializing in extraordinary feats of the mind and high emotional intelligence. My programs now include feats of memory that once seemed virtually impossible to me.

I now serve as a consultant and trainer to several business leaders, attorneys, medical practitioners, athletes, neuroscientists, and leaders in all walks of life. My passion has become working with our wounded warriors, and seniors with memory issues.

It has been an interesting journey and this book is my way of sharing the lessons I have learned.

I grew up in Allentown, Pennsylvania, one of four children, and after high school I attended Lehigh County Community College. I didn't do well in college, I spent most of my time in the dining hall playing cards, showing card tricks and playing chess. I never graduated from college and ended up working at the local steel mill.

It was at the steel mill that I earned the nickname "Magic" from my fellow steelworkers because of the various card tricks and stunts that I pulled on them. I would throw playing cards across the width of the mill and have contests with fellow employees to see who could throw cards the furthest. I would always look forward to working the night shift because my buddies and I would play poker and some of the games would last till the morning. Yeah, and no one would ever let me deal.

One night while playing cards, one of the guys told me about a fellow steel worker who owned a magic shop in Allentown called the Magic Den.

I met him the following week and he invited me to visit his shop. I had never been in a magic shop before, but after just one visit, I was like a kid in a candy store. I found a second home at the Magic Den every Saturday afternoon, meeting and learning from the area's top magicians.

Magic entered my life in more ways than one that year. I also met my wife Lynn, during the "steel mill" days. I remember trying to impress her one afternoon by trying to break a cement "cinder block" over my head. It must have worked! We got married the following year.

Shortly after we were married, I met the absolute most inspirational person of my life. He was an 80 year old performer at the Allentown Fair known as the Mighty Atom. At 5 feet 4 inches tall, and weighing in at 140 pounds, Atom stood in front of the crowd and took out a 60 penny nail (6 inch spike), and bent it in his bare hands!

Experiencing this THREE MINUTE DEMON-STRATION by this 80 year old MARVEL, left such an impact on me, that it changed my life forever!

Sure enough, after seeing the Mighty Atom, I just had to know how he performed that amazing feat of strength.

After numerous unsuccessful and painful attempts, I was about to give up.

However, I decided to give it one last shot, concentrating every ounce of mental energy. I was so focused that the thought of NOT bending it never even entered my mind.

All of a sudden, in an instant, the nail was bent. It felt like a stick of butter in my hands.

This was my very first lesson in emotional intelligence. NEVER GIVE UP!

I began bending spikes every day, just to work out. I gradually went up to 80 penny nails and my confidence and self-esteem rose through the roof – two more components of emotional intelligence. I didn't know at the time, but that was REALLY only the beginning!

Then all of a sudden, the steel mill began massive layoffs. Just like in the Billy Joel song "Allentown," many local residents lost their jobs, INCLUDING ME! I soon hit rock bottom financially. With a small child at home and another due any day, I tried desperately to find work, but nothing was available. With no job prospects, I took my wife's Avon account and went door-to-door selling Avon products. I livened up my presentations by doing card tricks. I don't know if the women felt sorry for me or liked my card tricks, but I became very successful selling Avon.

One day an Avon sales woman invited me to do a show in front of several hundred Avon women, and it went over really well. About a week later, I was asked to perform for a blue and gold Boy Scout banquet. I soon began performing for local companies and colleges, and appeared on several local news and television shows throwing cards, bending spikes and performing all sorts of tricks.

Word soon spread and before I knew it, I was performing magic shows throughout the northeast.

My dad loaned me some money to open up a magic shop of my own. I read every single book in the shop, including my two favorites, *How to Produce Miracles* by Ormond Mc Gill, and Corinda's *13 Steps to Mentalism*. I mastered EVERY trick in the store and really loved demonstrating the NEW tricks. Having the magic shop was EXTREMELY helpful in launching my new career.

I soon began performing at hundreds of colleges across the country. These appearances were always great fun and they will always be a part of what I do. I even wrote my first book back then, called "*50 Ways to Hustle Your Friends.*" That book became very popular on college campuses and I may bring that back in print some day!

I always included card throwing in the college shows and the students always wanted a demonstration. I would always hold card throwing contests and was urged by a number of students at several colleges to try to break the Guinness World record for long-distance throwing of a playing card. The world record was 155 feet, and I remembered throwing cards across the steel mill where we measured some of my tosses at 200 feet, so I thought, why not?

So on October 18, 1992, at Mt Ida College, outside of Boston, MA, I DID IT! I threw a standard bicycle playing card 201 feet to become the new Guinness World record holder.

That feat landed me on additional television shows, and, soon after, I was traveling across the country with several other Guinness record holders.

While out in Los Angeles attending a book expo to promote the Guinness Book of World Records Millennium Edition, I met a producer for the Rosie O'Donnell Show. I showed him the most unbelievable trick that he had ever seen. I had him pick a card and asked him to call my 8 year old son Justin.

After phoning Justin, the producer told Justin who he was and asked him to guess the card that he picked. When Justin correctly guessed the card, the producer dropped his cell phone and said "that's it, I want you on the show next week."

After performing on the Rosie O'Donnell show, things really started taking off. I began performing at bigger venues like the Trump Plaza in Atlantic City, where I did a show with a couple of friends and called it "Mind, Magic and Madness."

The most important part of my story about "The Evolution of Jim Karol," didn't begin until the age of 49.

About two weeks before my 50th birthday, I began to experience chest pains. I was overweight and out of shape but was not prepared for the diagnosis that I was about to receive. I was told that I had cardiomyopathy, and had the heartbeat of a 90-year-old person. I guess the 21 quarts of milk a week and thousands of cheese steaks and cheese dogs finally caught up with me. Being on the road all the time and eating a dozen donuts a week didn't help much either!

When I was leaving the doctor's office, I asked him for some advice, and he said "enjoy the ride."

That wasn't the answer that I was looking for.

I went home, and I remember telling my wife Lynn, "That's it." "No more cheese steaks." "No more cheese dogs." I began eating nothing but salads and chicken and started riding an exercise bike in my basement, beginning the long road back to good health.

Now, riding an exercise bike can become really boring. That's why I began doing the memory feats described throughout this book.

The first thing I tried was to see how fast I could memorize a shuffled deck of cards. Then I began memorizing countries, capitals, digits of pi, sporting events, Oscar winners and anything else I could get my hands on.

After a while, time began to fly by quickly, and I was doing 30 miles on the bike like it was nothing and working my brain at the same time.

I was nailing down 100 digits of Pi a day and feeling absolutely amazing.

While riding my exercise bike, I also memorized almost ALL of the U.S. zip codes, every word in the Scrabble dictionary, all the Oscar winners, football hall of famers, baseball hall of famers, countries, capitals, almanacs and thousands of other facts.

I ended up dropping 40 pounds and felt better than ever. After a while, I began incorporating all my new found memory feats into my show.

Ten years later I was turning 60 and my life insurance was up for renewal. They turned me down because of the heart condition, so I asked my doctor if I could get the echocardiogram again. When I walked in the room for the echo test, it was the same technician that I had 10 years earlier. He complimented me, telling me I looked younger than I did 10 years ago. They then gave me the incredible news that I no longer had cardiomyopathy.

He told me to just keep doing whatever I was doing because it was working. That really motivated me to turn my energy up a few notches MORE. I turned up the brain workout to several hours a day and began lifting weights again like I was 25 years old.

Having put the medical issues behind me, I accelerated my learning curve.

In the past two years I have moved way beyond lists of countries, movie stars and athletes. I now research and study the brain and medical terms. Things like the skeletal system, neurons, the cranial nerves,

neurotransmitters, emotional intelligence and neuroscience have all become a part of my daily routine.

I began to realize that the things I was doing were
made possible, in large part, by the presence and application of emotional intelligence. The combination of
everything that I've done over the last 12 years, has
given me higher emotional intelligence and has definitely
improved my brain health and wellness.

A chapter of this book is devoted to poker. There
is a reason for that.

I spent, and still do spend, a lot of time playing
poker. I have studied every aspect of the game for years.
I am convinced that poker is a great asset in developing
heightened emotional intelligence.

It also became obvious that memory, focus, intuition, poker and other mind games could all play a role
in developing HEIGHTENED emotional intelligence.

This became my compelling area of concentration.
I now believe that passion, positive energy and a happy
attitude can help overcome almost anything. I also
believe that it doesn't matter if you are 6 years old or
86 years old, you can still improve your memory and
quality of health.

Teaching the world how to achieve heightened
emotional intelligence and improve their brain wellness is my mission, even if it's only ONE PERSON AT
A TIME!

Chapter 2

The Magnificent Brain
Era of the Brain

"The chief function of the BODY,
is to carry the BRAIN around." —Thomas Edison

Emotions emanate from the brain. This is a book about increasing your emotional intelligence and brain wellness. The book would not be complete without understanding the basics of how we, as individuals, can control our brain, and, thereby, increase our emotional intelligence.

The HUMAN BRAIN is absolutely magnificent! Weighing in at about three pounds, the brain controls our thoughts, our intelligence, our emotions, our vital organs, our heart rate, breathing and thousands of other functions.

Brain study is becoming a major focus of governments around the world. Publications of varying focus offer a steady stream of articles examining functions of the brain.

The brain receives information through our senses: sight, smell, touch, taste, and hearing. It then distributes the received messages throughout the cortex and sub cortex. Everyone could benefit greatly from basic brain knowledge. It would be cool if Neurons 101, Brain Cells 101, would become basic educational courses.

Learning the terms describing brain structure and physiology were extremely helpful in increasing my emotional intelligence. (See Appendix A for more detailed information on brain structures and functions)

If you exercise daily and eat healthy, you will look good, feel better and have a healthier body. The same works for the brain. If you exercise your brain daily and eat healthy, you will feel better, focus more clearly and have a healthier mind!

Having a healthy body AND a healthy mind, truly maximizes your LIFE.

The brain tends to stick with familiar solutions and fails to recognize alternatives unless it is challenged.

Clayton Christensen of the Harvard business school wrote:

"Disruptive technologies introduce a very different package of attributes from the one mainstream customers historically use. Concentration on brain study and applying new knowledge is the ultimate disruptive technology."

I believe, that concentrated exercise, better nutrition and positive attitude, contributed in helping my heart problem.

Many medical experts who I have worked with, now accept as a fact that plaque and clogged arteries are a primary cause of heart attacks and strokes. Regular exercise has proven, not just for me, but for millions, to be a magic potion for clearing arteries, restoring and maintaining heart health and extending longevity.

Many of these same medical experts and their colleagues are now focusing on plaque in the clogging of pathways in the brain as a suspect in all forms of dementia, including Alzheimer's. As diagnostic advances are made, many medical practitioners feel that we will prove a direct connection between the accumulation of brain plaque and the threat of memory loss.

I believe that in the next few years, "brain exercise" prescriptions will be as common and effective as those physical exercise programs prescribed now to conquer heart problems. One of my more extreme brain wellness exercises is set out as Appendix B.

We have learned more about the brain in the last 15 years than the ENTIRE history of the world. We continue to learn at an accelerated pace. Just think where we will be in ANOTHER 15 years?

Why wait? Get ahead of the curve. Improve your mind functions with a regular program of physical exercise. Then augment the program with daily brain exercises. The programs for your brain should never get stale. They must change just as the physical exercises change for your body.

As we age, and, as a result of inattention, we lose many of our brain connections AND neurons. This does not have to be a one way street. We can create new connections AND new neurons through our own efforts.

This is where emotional intelligence comes in. The higher our emotional intelligence, the more likely we are to do what is necessary to maintain a growing, effectively functioning brain. The more we do mental exercises and strive to keep our brains healthy the more likely we are to have heightened emotional intelligence. This book is designed to help you make the connection between the healthy functioning of your brain and heightened emotional intelligence.

Intellectual challenges stimulate the brain to make more connections, just as doing barbell curls give you bigger biceps. The more connections we have in our brains, the more resilient the brain.

FOCUS... You will see that word a lot throughout this book. Focus on brain training and make it an essential part of your life. Make it fun, and also make it challenging.

The era of the brain promises to be the most rewarding in all of human history.

Come along for the journey. Be an active participant!

Amazing Brain Facts

- New brain connections are created every time you form a new memory. When you learn new things, the structure of your brain changes.

- Your brain has enough ENERGY to power a light bulb. Your brain can retain TRILLIONS of pieces of information. The average brain has 70,000 thoughts per day.

– Listening to music strengthens the brain.

– With daily MENTAL exercise, the Brain continues to make new neurons throughout our lives.

– Yawning, sends MORE oxygen to the brain.

– Excessive STRESS has shown to alter brain cells and brain function.

Chapter 3

Emotional Intelligence

*"I have no special talents, I am only
passionately curious." —Albert Einstein*

What is emotional intelligence?

There are numerous interpretations of the term "emotional intelligence."

Psychology Today provides an interesting definition:

*Emotional intelligence is generally said to include
THREE skills:*

1. *Emotional awareness, including the ability to
   identify your own emotions and those of others;*
2. *The ability to harness emotions and apply them
   to tasks like thinking and problem solving;*
3. *The ability to regulate your own emotions with the
   ability to cheer up or calm down another person.*

An article published by the University of New Hampshire offers the following:

> *... The meaning of emotional intelligence has something specific to do with the intelligent intersection of the emotions and thoughts. For example, emotional intelligence represents an ability to validly reason with emotions and to use emotions to enhance thought.*

What an empowering concept! The same article continues with a more formal definition:

> *We define EI (emotional intelligence is also abbreviated as EQ) as the capacity to reason about emotions, and of emotions to enhance thinking. It includes the abilities to accurately perceive emotions, to access and generate emotions so as to assist thought, to understand emotions and emotional knowledge and to reflectively regulate emotions so as to promote emotional and intellectual growth.*

Clearly, a person who has developed these skills has a powerful advantage over their peers whatever their chosen field may be.

MY favorite definition of emotional intelligence is "the uncanny ability to accurately analyze the non-verbal clues that people send out." I have been doing this in my show for more than 30 years and have become pretty good at it. Once you are able to read someone, it is much easier to communicate, and determine their emotional state as well.

The ability to read the poker tells of a competitive player, the trust of a business adversary, or the mood of a date, are all part of emotional intelligence. This "reading people" skill can be taught. It can be easily learned, and can also be constantly upgraded and refined. To achieve mastery, as with all skills, it requires constant PRACTICE and dedication.

I always look forward to the presidential debates on TV. It is a great way for me to "brush up" on reading the "TELLS" of the candidates.

I used to love watching witnesses on Court TV testify under oath as well. I would focus, study and practice reading people and have developed an ability to separate truth from deceit and lies.

People with high emotional intelligence don't just control their own emotions effectively and accurately, they can also interpret the body language and verbal clues emitted by others and can take it to another level. Some people with high emotional intelligence even seem to have a magical influence on people, by having the ability to attract them into their world.

One other key element of true emotional intelligence is being capable of managing and controlling your OWN emotions and actions. This is an area where I still need some work and improvement.

My temper was a lot worse when I was younger, but has improved greatly since I began working on my emotional intelligence. The sooner you get a hold on your own emotions, the better. Every morning I wake up with the goal of trying to be a little more positive. Attaining high emotional intelligence is a quest and a journey with hills, valleys, nooks and crannies. Keeping at it, however, may lead you to excellence!

Striving for excellence requires high emotional intelligence, positive attitude, strong will and passion.

Getting back to emotions and stress. The best area to start the process of enhancing emotional intelligence is by effectively handing stress and moods. In the last two years, I have learned to use emotional intelligence to rapidly convert my stress into energy. The longer that you continue to be stressed, the more likely negative change will begin to occur. You must try to get out of bad moods as soon as possible!

Effective stress management is a powerful expression of emotional intelligence.

Our brain is capable of handling stress for a short period of time, but long, unabated stress can have debilitating effects on us physically and mentally.

As you progress, you will not only be able to short-circuit your own stressful expressions, but you will also be a source of stress relief for those who come in contact with you. This is part of the charismatic impact you will have on others. When we meet each other, we instantly check each other out. It's a natural human instinct, part of the law of attraction. We can easily affect each other by the way we talk and by the way we look. People with higher emotional intelligence will clearly have an advantage in these situations.

When I am performing or speaking, I am constantly checking out my audience, looking for certain people and personalities to pull up on stage. Any magician or mentalist can benefit greatly from heightened emotional intelligence.

It will definitely make you a better performer by being able to read your audience and better connect with them.

Another area where high EQ can come in handy is with trial lawyers. If a trial lawyer has good emotional intelligence, they are more likely to be a much better trial lawyer. At the same time, trying numerous cases over and over, will also enhance the emotional intelligence of the lawyer.

This happens because you are constantly reading people in the courtroom which can be very stressful, and the ability to control that stress and deal with it is a major part of what emotional intelligence is all about. A person with high EQ is always LISTENING! They know that what you HEAR, is more important than what you say.

Steve Martin, the comedian, actor, and magician is a great example. He offered his view that we should not just listen with our ears or even our eyes. We should "listen" with all of our senses and absorb all of the messages being sent by our audiences and respond accordingly.

If you do that, you are far more likely to be a successful performer. If you lack that quality or ability you're never really going to be successful.

When you're talking, you're sending out signals and information in words, but if you're not RECEIVING back, your performance is falling short of what it could be.

Steve Martin's advice offers a wonderful lesson in the practical use of emotional intelligence.

He makes clear that a critical step in improving your emotional intelligence is to REALLY LISTEN to people. Listen with ALL of your senses! That alone will set you apart because most people don't really ever listen. Some people can't wait for their turn to talk. They can't wait for the speaker to be done, because they just want to be the one talking. Some people just don't focus or pay attention.

ALWAYS be a good listener. That alone will contribute a lot to building better relationships with people. It is also an important early step on the emotional intelligence road to progress.

Let me share with you some important benefits you get from having enhanced emotional intelligence:

a) It will enhance your life personally and professionally.

b) It will help you build much stronger relationships.

c) It will greatly improve your communication skills.

d) It will increase your energy, memory and knowledge.

e) It will give you more self-esteem.

f) It will help you manage stress.

THE KEYS TO UNLOCKING YOUR EMOTIONAL INTELLIGENCE

Positive Thought

You must gradually eliminate ALL negative thought and emotion. This may sound difficult for some people. Like I said, I am still working on that area myself. The more that you surround yourself with positive people and positive influence, the more positive you will become.

Exercise (Physical & Mental)

Beginning a daily exercise routine not only helps you physically, but will also help you reduce stress. I take it a step further by exercising my MIND each day as well. I can tell you from firsthand experience, that exercising your mind and body are the most pivotal things that you can do for your overall health!

Confidence

Developing confidence in yourself plays a HUGE role in boosting your EQ. I was always shy and backwards and had almost ZERO confidence when I was in high school. I began getting more confidence in myself by showing card tricks. After seeing the reaction on people's faces, it began giving me the boost that I needed.

It's working the same for me today with memory. The look that I get when I recite zip codes or Oscar winners, keeps MY confidence boosted.

Poker

You may be wondering why Poker is on this list. Playing poker sharpens your ability to read body language, teaches you how to handle stress and enhances your social skills. I've been playing cards for more than 40 years, and I can assure you that EQ and card games like poker, pinochle and bridge, all go hand in hand. As you become a better card player, that also gives your confidence a boost.

Focus

In my opinion, Focus is the most important component to achieving higher emotional intelligence. I like to play chess to strengthen my focus. If you ever played chess, you know how important it is to stay focused. If you let your mind drift for even a minute or two, the game can be over very quickly!

Failure Is a Part of Success

Learn how to bounce back from adversity. Failure "IS" acceptable, but ONLY if you learn from it. Move on from failure, BELIEVE in yourself and know that failure is a part of success. Be courageous and keep moving ahead!

Memory

Improving your memory will definitely help you achieve higher emotional intelligence. This isn't just talk, it really, REALLY works! Check out my chapter on memory in this book.

Really Listen

Like I said earlier in this chapter, most people don't really listen. If you're talking, you're not really listening. Learning how to listen with empathy, will put you on the road to higher emotional intelligence.

Self Awareness

Self-awareness is having the knowledge and aware-ness of your own individuality. I have found that logging my thoughts and daily experiences in my smart phone, really helped me in getting to know myself better.

Self Control

It is very important to learn how to manage and control your OWN thoughts and emotions, and how to handle criticism. When I talk out loud to myself, it actually changes my mood and actions. Always STOP and THINK before you act, and most of all, NEVER lose your cool!

Here are a few more helpful ideas:

Meditation

There are mountains of books written about the benefits of meditation. Clearly, making meditation a daily practice will help enhance your emotional intelligence by making space in your brain for peace and quiet. I have learned to meditate and to drop into a deep state of concentration while doing memorization work. I like to call it "memitation."

Building Stronger Relationships

This not only applies to personal friendships, but also applies to customer relationships, diplomatic negotiations, gamesmanship and marriage.

I have been happily married to my wife Lynn for 38 years. I firmly believe that following the guidelines to higher EQ, contributed greatly. I hope to one day have the high emotional intelligence that Lynn has!

Positive Belief

The single most important trait of successful people, in virtually every field, is POSITIVE belief, or, to use the more common term, high self-esteem. If you don't believe in yourself, the odds are that others will doubt you as well. High self-esteem radiates an aura of attraction. Heightened emotional intelligence is certain to increase your self-esteem.

When I was young I was bullied at school. I never wanted to speak in front of the class. I was shy and backward in all my personal relationships and had virtually no self-esteem. My grades were terrible and I felt like that all through high school.

Everything changed when I began doing magic. The excitement and joy in everyone's faces gave me an immediate boost of confidence.

My confidence began to grow and grow. I am not kidding when I say a deck of cards saved my life. I began to develop a powerful image of myself and a much more positive attitude. I began to look people in the eye, which I had never done before. This was the beginning of MY journey to achieving higher emotional intelligence. Learning magic definitely helped me improve my self-esteem.

Intuition

Increase the accuracy of your intuition. Intuition is the term for "gut feeling" or something that you know, or think likely, based on instinctive feeling rather than conscious reasoning. When you get an instant feeling of liking or disliking someone you just met, that is your intuition telling you. Your intuition can also give you a "heads up" when something good or bad is about to happen.

Intuition is the ability to process information quickly, and can easily be developed by observing people and things closely. It is critical to use all of your senses in the observation process. Keep in mind that intuition is an important aspect of emotional intelligence. The accuracy and strength of your intuition grows, with repeated exposure to situations and their outcomes.

If you pay attention to your feelings and surroundings, you will often be guided by an INTUITIVE feeling. You may not recall when the initial thought occurred. Odds are that grabbing on to the intuitive feeling will come a moment when you focused. You will gradually learn how to respond and react to different situations. The more you practice observing and listening, the more intuitive you will become.

Dreams are extremely important to enhancing your intuition as well. Many famous inventors discovered great ideas in their dreams.

Paul McCartney had a dream which became the hit song, "Yesterday." Mary Shelley's "Frankenstein" was inspired by a dream.

Elias Howe invented the sewing machine after a vivid dream.

Einstein's world changing theory of relativity began as a dream.

Always keep a recorder or a pad and pen next to your bed to capture important dreams when you wake up during the night.

My OWN "222" dream was a life-changing event for me. (See Appendix C). I'm glad there was a pen and pad next to me when I woke up during the night. Without writing down my 222 dream I would never have remembered it. Despite the headline, I am NOT a psychic and have never claimed to be a psychic. I did have the dream, however, and it seemed VERY real and came true!

You are off to a good start. You have learned what emotional intelligence is. You have a starting point for recognizing and measuring the benefits available to you.

Focus, work hard, concentrate and listen to yourself. In the course of pursuing the benefits of emotional intelligence you will discover what works best for you.

It is also important to remember that this is a dynamic and never ending process.

You will get better and better each month.

Stay with it and you will change your life for the better.

Remember to:

Always be confident and cheerful.

Always be positive and energetic.

Always be complimentary and kind.

Always be gracious.

Most of all, ALWAYS keep your cool!

People who can benefit GREATLY from higher emotional intelligence:

- Law Enforcement Officers
- Teachers
- Military
- Medical and Healthcare
- Firefighters
- Flight Attendants
- Politicians
- Poker players
- Performers
- Attorneys
- Judges
- Salespeople
- Reporters
- CEO's
- Athletes and Coaching staff

How about EVERYBODY?!?

Chapter 4

Emotional Intelligence in Action

"All that we are is the result of what we have thought."
—Buddha

I have worked with a number of people with issues ranging from poor memory to PTSD. I have no medical training and don't claim to have medical answers to complex health issues. However, I've been able to help many people with my magic, memory training and by introducing them to emotional intelligence.

Asperger's syndrome is considered to be a part of the autism spectrum. Many people with Asperger's can have a difficult time with social interactions as well as interactions with their family and fellow workers. This can lead to frustration, withdrawal and loneliness.

Jason (whose name has been changed) was a typical young boy with Asperger's. He, like many others, wanted to interact with family and to make friends, but found both to be difficult for him.

I was invited by Jason's dad to visit their home in Florida and spend some time with Jason. When I first met Jason, he was spinning a globe, and I asked him if he knew any of the countries on the globe? He proudly pointed and said "this is Canada, this is Mexico, this is where WE live," pointing to the U.S. I asked him if he knew the capital of Canada, and when I told him it was Ottawa, he smiled and said "you're right." Then I asked him to point to ANY country on the globe and he pointed to Madagascar. When I told him the capital was Antananarivo, the look on his face was "priceless" and I knew that I had found Jason's "IT." The word "IT" is a term that I like to use when I really connect with someone. I continued guessing capitals and showed Jason several magic tricks. We had a great time.

He asked me to teach him a few magic tricks and countries and their capitals as well. Jason became really excited as he learned many new countries like France, Russia, Germany, England and also their capitals. The more countries and capitals that he learned, the happier he became.

Believe it or not, after spending just two days with Jason and his family, Jason learned more than 100 countries and the capitals.

His dad recently called me and said that Jason NOW knows all 212 countries and capitals. He told me that when he asked Jason, "What the capital of South Africa was?"

Jason looked him in the eye and with a smile on his face said, "which one do you want Dad, Cape Town, Pretoria or Bloemfontein?"

I have had similar experiences with several individuals using the idea and application of magic, memory and emotional intelligence.

I met a high school Principal at a presentation I was making. He approached me after the meeting and asked if I would do him a favor.

He explained that a number of the 10th grade students in his school were struggling and their grades were really dropping, and wanted to know if I would be able to meet with them one evening when I was available.

I agreed to come to the school the following week. He invited about 20 students and their parents and we called it an evening of magic and memory.

When I got there, I was surprised to see that everyone had showed up. Some of them were slumped in their chairs making it clear that they did not want to be there, but I was just glad that they showed up.

The Principal set the stage by telling them they were all there because he believed in them and in their potential to succeed, not just in school, but in life. He created a favorable and positive atmosphere before introducing me.

I began by doing a magic trick and some of the students recognized me from TV. A few remained skeptical, but most of them began to sit up in their chairs and listen to what I had to say. I showed a few more really cool tricks and gradually won everyone over. I then showed them how to do a magic trick and they wanted to see more. That's when I knew that I found their "IT."

When I asked them to raise their hand if they were failing History, all 20 hands went up. I wanted to teach them something that would be both entertaining and also had something to do with history.

I once developed a memory routine that made it easy to learn the U.S. presidents, so I decided that it would be a perfect fit for this group. The president "trick" is not only fun and entertaining, but baffles the mind as well.

I wrote the names of all the past presidents on the blackboard and after showing them the routine, they all wanted to learn it.

I told the students that if they learned the names of the first 10 presidents in order and came into the

Principal's office the next morning and recited the names they could get a DVD showing them how to do the 12 magic tricks that I showed them.

Jim Karol's Cool Card Tricks was a DVD that I had developed with the United States Playing Card Company a few years ago. I still had a hundred or so left at home and told the principal I would get them to him if any of the students were successful.

The next morning I received a phone call from my principal friend. At first, he laughed. Then he said, "Jim, do you have 21 copies of those DVDs?"

All 20 kids came into his office one at a time, recited the presidents from memory and asked for a copy of the DVD. He also wanted one for himself.

The story gets better. After two years, the principal followed up and told me that all 20 students graduated from high school and several were going off to college.

Emotional intelligence can be a powerful force when used for good!

I remember the first time that I heard about Walter Reed Army Medical Center. My wife Lynn, was watching the Oprah Show, when Oprah was on location at Walter Reed in February of 2009. Lynn was so emotional after watching the show and suggested that I should visit Walter Reed. I tried contacting several entertainment agents about it, with no luck.

Then about two months later, I was playing in a charity poker tournament outside of Boston, and I met Montel Williams. I had appeared on his television show back in 1999 to promote the Millennium Edition of the Guinness Book of Records for which I had two records.

Montel is very caring for our wounded service men and women and one of the coolest people I have ever met. One day he asked me if I wanted to accompany him to Walter Reed and entertain everyone with my magic performance. When I told my wife, she was really excited that I finally found a way to perform there.

That first visit changed my life forever! I had been performing for more than 20 years, at more than 2,000 colleges, and nothing can even come close to how it felt to perform for the young men and women who were at Walter Reed. I knew immediately, that my magic now had a purpose. I met some super and amazing people that day, including some very special people from the USO.

A couple of months later, Montel invited me to join him again, and I jumped at the chance. Everyone knew Montel. He was like a rock star down there and it was an honor to travel with him. On this particular trip, we visited some of the wounded warriors in their hospital rooms. I will never forget the reaction and the look on some of their faces and the honor it was for me, to have the opportunity to perform for TRUE AMERICAN HEROES!

I met a young lady that day named Pauline, who worked with the USO. Pauline and everyone else with the USO, I've had the pleasure to work with, are absolutely fantastic, caring people.

Talk about emotional intelligence, the incredible work that Pauline and her associates do, exemplifies high emotional intelligence!

Pauline has brought me back numerous times and recently the USO and I have put together a program that teaches memory skills, emotional intelligence and even some card tricks.

I look forward to going there each month and wouldn't be surprised to see one of these young men or women on America's Got Talent one day.

Everywhere that I appear now, people are always asking me if I can help them with their memory and Emotional Intelligence, and I love it!

I will tell you this, since traveling to Walter Reed and Fort Belvoir on a regular basis, my own emotional intelligence has definitely improved greatly.

I am currently in the process of developing a one hour program designed to help college students across the country. After being a college entertainer for more than 30 years, I learned how college students think, and what they are looking for.

My program will combine cognitive fitness, memory training and advanced emotional intelligence. It will be fun and entertaining as well, and will change people's lives like it did for me.

The program will also be adapted for BABY BOOMERS across the country. I definitely want to reach the people who think that their brain goes downhill after the age of 55.

I can tell you from experience, that if you follow the basic examples and tips set forth in the last two chapters, and stick with it on a regular basis, people close to you will see dramatic changes in YOU!

The most important things are to:

Stay FOCUSED
Really listen
Maintain self-control
EXERCISE physically and mentally

One of the most effective ways to go BEYOND enhanced emotional intelligence, is to reach out to those in need.

Chapter 5

Focus

"The successful warrior is the average man with laser like FOCUS."—Bruce Lee

FOCUS, is the key to memory, learning, education, understanding, knowledge, and much more!

If that sounds pretty important, that's because IT IS!

Without focus and concentration, it would be nearly impossible to learn.

It would be like an average person trying to read a book in a loud dance club, with bright colored lights flashing to the beat of the music.

Distraction is the number one deterrent to focus and concentration. Think about the big difference between walking down Broadway in Times Square, with all the taxi's, bright lights, sirens and people, compared to walking along a quiet beach on a tropical island at sunset.

If you learn to focus properly, you will begin to see things that you never knew were there.

People are constantly telling me that they have a poor memory or their memory is deteriorating. In most cases, it's not their memory, it's because they're not focused!

As you're parking your car at the mall, you get a call on your cell phone. You start talking to someone, shut off your car and head into the mall, still talking.

You're walking around looking in a few store windows and are still talking on the phone.

You have a million things on your mind. Now after a quick lunch you leave and realize that you forgot where you parked the car.

Guess what? You didn't forget where you parked the car. Your memory is not slipping. It has to do with FOCUS! You weren't focused when you were getting out of the car, you were on the phone and very distracted. That's most likely the reason why you couldn't find your car.

This actually just happened to me recently.

I was in Orlando doing a Brain Boot Camp at Florida Hospital with Tony Dottino, the founder of the USA Memory Championship. After the session, we went to Universal Studios for dinner. As Tony was parking the car, we were both on our cell phones, not FOCUSING on where we parked. After having dinner and doing some shopping, we walked back to the parking lot and neither one of us could remember where we parked. Here you have two of the "so called" best memory guys in the world, and we didn't have a clue where we parked. Don't get me wrong, Universal Studio's parking lot is huge, but it should not have taken the two of us over an hour to find the car! It wasn't because we had a bad memory, it was simply because neither one of us was focused when we were parking the car.

People have a few experiences with losing keys, forgetting a name or missing a detail on something they are doing. They then start saying to themselves, "I have a bad memory," and before long it becomes a self-fulfilling prophecy.

When you think and tell yourself that you have a bad memory, then before long, you may have a bad memory. To avoid having that happen you simply focus on what you are doing. Learn to live in the moment, and do everything possible to utilize your emotional intelligence.

Focus and memory are two totally different forms of cognitive function, but they're extremely important to each other. Focus is how you improve your memory. Without deep focus you will have difficulty with any type of memorization. If I'm trying to teach you how to memorize something and your mind has drifted and you're not focused on what I'm trying to teach you, you're not going to have a good memory experience.

Focus and memory go hand in hand. That's often the problem. There is a disconnect in your memory efforts when you are not focused. If students are not focused and not alert and not paying attention they will remember very little of what they were taught. It's not that they really don't remember what was taught. The fact is that they never paid attention and never learned it in the first place.

Now, when I think back to my high school days, I am 100% sure that I didn't do well because I NEVER focused or paid attention, and didn't want to be there.

My mind was everywhere else BUT school.

Focus is a key to learning and achieving higher emotional intelligence. The same is true with memory and with cognitive fitness. These practices and attributes are all closely linked together. Without focus, we find ourselves meandering through life. Our memory will suffer. Our cognitive fitness will suffer. Focus is the binding solution that holds it all together.

Everything begins with a new idea. Then comes focus. With focus, your new idea can find wings. Focus allows the idea we hold in our conscious to be an object of passionate concentration.

I'll never forget my first appearance on the Tonight Show. I actually had a dream in December 2001 that I appeared on the Tonight Show with Johnny Carson. I did this really cool card trick where Johnny picked a card, then turned on a television and the Letterman Show was on. I was a guest on Letterman and pulled a card out of my pocket and said "this is your card Johnny, the 2 of hearts!" Then I woke up. Eleven months later I appeared on the Tonight Show, but the host wasn't Johnny, it was Jay Leno. So my dream "kind of" came true.

During my REAL appearance on Leno, I was supposed to place my hand in a fox trap. While out in Los Angeles, I purchased a much bigger trap, which happened to be a bear trap. I didn't plan on using the bear trap for the Tonight Show, but when the producer saw it, he insisted that I use the BIGGER trap. I remember him saying to me "bigger is better for television."

During rehearsal, I asked them to find me a thick glove, to try it out. When I placed my hand in the trap for the very first time, it hurt like hell, even with the thick glove on. Then one of the producers asked if I could do it again, so that she could get a better camera angle. I said "No way," it hurt way too much, and I wasn't sure if I wanted to do it at all. I talked them into waiting until my LIVE appearance to do it again, but only if I could wear the glove.

When Jay finally introduced me that was the very first time that I was ever nervous before a show. I was about to stick my hand in a bear trap, and my hand was still thumping from rehearsal. As soon as I came out from behind the curtain, my butterflies instantly disappeared. I got my mental FOCUS back and realized that I was on the Tonight Show, in front of millions of people. That was something that I had truly dreamed of, so I just focused on the moment.

Jay was briefly interviewing me about my life as a steel worker and some of the crazy things that I had done in the past. He really made me feel comfortable, and after about five minutes, we got into my stunt. The segment was called "Don't Try This At Home."

I demonstrated that the trap was indeed REAL, by placing a beer bottle in it. Jay and I wore goggles, and the first 10 rows of the audience held up a huge sheet of clear plastic to protect themselves from flying debris. After the trap shattered the bottle, pieces flew all the way back to the rear of the studio.

As I was about to stick my hand in the trap, I ripped off the glove and decided, last second, to do it BARE HANDED!

I had absolutely no idea what was going to happen when I jammed my hand into that huge trap, but I was SOOOO FOCUSED, that negativity never entered my mind.

When the trap snapped on my hand, I felt no pain whatsoever. I could not believe how powerful positive thought and mental focus could be. The audience went crazy and I learned a huge lesson about FOCUS!

The power of the Human Mind is absolutely amazing!

Here is a list of steps which will help you focus:

1. When you are engaging in a conversation, a meeting, watching a performance, putting on a performance or playing a competitive game, "LISTEN" with all your senses.

    Also "listen" to yourself with all your senses. Listen just as attentively to yourself, to your innermost feelings and to your intentions as you listen to others and to what is going on around you.

2. Look people in the eye when you are communicating with them. Pay attention. Listen closely, and if you didn't hear them clearly, never hesitate to ask them to repeat what they said, especially if it is the pronunciation of their name. Repeating something helps you focus and remember much better.

3. Always try to focus on one thing at a time. You can never effectively process everything going on around you at once. Focus, by focusing! Don't multi-task!

4. Always have a sincere intention to hear and understand.

    React physically to what you see, hear and are taking in. This emotional involvement will increase your likelihood of retaining the memory.

5. Concentrate. Don't think about what you are going to say while you are listening.

6. Don't pretend to understand if you really did not. Ask questions. Be interested. Don't hesitate to say I don't know. That sentence will lead to a lifetime of learning.

Numerous studies show (no surprise) that those who are FOCUSED produce better results in virtually every instance. Extended tests make it clear that those who are committed to a positive result (i.e., are highly motivated or inspired) will have far better focus and will almost always produce better results.

The biggest battle that many of us have in life, is the war within – the conflict between what we say we want and what we actually do. This is the ongoing battle between living the life others want us to have and what our subconscious mind says we should be living.

Many of us fear failure, we miss the great opportunities in our life that we say we are passionate about.

Write down what you are truly passionate about, then FOCUS on it intently.

It can provide a window to look into your future. If you want to see your future, simply look at the thoughts that dominate your thinking today.

Are those thoughts programming you to get where you want to go? If not, you need to turn up the volume on your emotional intelligence. You need to begin a transformational process which will allow you to control those thoughts rather than you being controlled by them. You need to FOCUS.

One of the BEST things that I do to increase my focus, is play a game of CHESS or even CHECKERS!

I'll never forget the time back on November 14, 1997. I was at Springfield College in Springfield, Mass. I was attempting to break another Guinness World Record for checkers. The previous record was 172 consecutive opponents without a loss or draw. I beat the record that night by defeating 180 consecutive college students and professors. Talk about FOCUS! If I would have lost focus for even one minute, I may have lost a game, especially since these were very BRIGHT opponents that I played against. My focus probably tripled that night. While driving home, it began to snow and the snowflakes looked like big white checkers falling from the sky. I played checkers and stayed focused for SEVEN HOURS that night!

Back in the beginning of this chapter, I used the analogies about the average person trying to read a book in a very loud dance club and walking down Broadway in Times Square with the bright colored billboards, the sirens blaring, the taxis honking their horns and thousands of people. Well guess what? Once you learn how to MASTER your focus, you will also learn how to block out ALL distractions and ZONE INTO THE MOMENT, no matter where you are!

I often go to Times Square and other noisy areas, just to challenge my focus and make it even STRONGER!

Ringo Starr famously said "you must either kiss goodbye your past or your future." That statement indicated that he possessed high emotional intelligence. You can't create the future you want or enjoy the present moment you are living in, if your thoughts are dominated by past experiences.

Stay focused on your goals. Picture the end result and all the satisfaction it will bring.

Chapter 6

Reading People

"When the eyes say one thing, and the tongue another,
a practiced man relies on the language of the first."
—Ralph Waldo Emerson

This is my favorite chapter in the book and the main reason that I became interested in emotional intelligence.

Reading the body language and tells of people has been a specialty of mine since getting into the entertainment business 30 years ago. These skills and abilities have gotten stronger over the years, and the more that I exercise my brain, the more powerful the ability becomes.

I would practice by playing poker whenever I performed near a casino. When a player looked at their cards, I would look at their eyes and face, to watch for clues. In more cases than not, there was a discernible expression that was visible to read. It was usually either an expression of excitement or an expression of "damn!"

Anyone can see the expressions if they know what to look for, but it usually happens very quickly, sometimes in less than a second.

Today, with TV broadcasts of Texas Hold 'em, you get to see the two cards that each player is dealt. You can then instantly compare that with your reading of the person, and know if you were correct.

After a while, relating poker and emotional intelligence came naturally for me. I had been a casual poker player most of my life. However, as I began to take the game more seriously, I realized that there was an edge and a skill involved, that it wasn't just about luck.

I was fascinated by the prospect of elevating this skill, and began playing poker on a daily basis.

My study of poker and emotional intelligence led to watching the best poker players in the world who played nightly in numerous tournaments covered on cable television.

I would watch for hours just for practice. Once I even taped the final table of an event and slowed down the recording. It's amazing how much more you see by simply slowing down the video and showing it frame by frame.

The television coverage of poker events was, and still is, fantastic. You can see a player's reaction to the cards they are dealt and then see the cards they are holding.

Patterns of reactions could be seen quickly, even when watching some of the most skilled players.

There were tells buried in their eyes, their facial expressions and the movements of their hands.

The word TELL has a special meaning in the poker world. A tell is a change in a player's demeanor which gives clues to the strength or weakness of a player's hand.

Players who successfully read the tells of their opponents gain a huge advantage. There is a never ending debate as to whether poker is more a game of luck or a game of skill. One thing is for sure – those players who have a heightened ability (skill) to read and understand the meaning of their opponents' tells definitely have a substantial advantage.

I really wanted to go deeper into reading the eyes and other messages people were sending out. I wanted to read people in EVERY walk of life. So I started watching the news, NOT for current events, but to practice reading the tells of guests. I still watch CNN and Fox. The lessons are invaluable.

I enjoy watching Bill O'Reilly just to study those who present differing points of view, just as I had done with poker players. I study the EYES and mannerisms of his guests, especially the one's who have an opposite point of view to Bill O'Reilly.

Being able to do that, is what emotional intelligence is all about to me.

I've literally watched thousands of faces. You can't just watch one or two people and think that you know how to read people. It has become a POSITIVE obsession for me!

I have spent years reading eyes in my career. I've made over 3,000 appearances at colleges across the country, and students always came up to me after my show and asked me to look into their eyes. Everyone is always trying to test me out and stump me.

That alone, keeps me on my toes and is great PRACTICE.

My favorite example is to ask someone a series of questions and have them answer "NO" to every question, no matter what I ask.

I then tell them in response to every question whether or not they were answering truthfully. I've done that thousands and thousands of times. I can't believe how accurate I've become since I started.

Here are a few tips of things that can be used to spot a lie:

Tip number one to spot a lie is to watch for a SLIGHT BLUSHING.

I once played in a private poker game. I can't mention where or who was playing. I was paid to be there to observe one of the players, in particular, to see if they were cheating. Someone paid me to observe the action and paid my entrance fee. If I won any money I got to keep it, but I really wasn't there to win money. I was there to try to catch a cheater.

Around midnight after we had been playing for several hours we took a break to order pizza. This guy (Joe) came up to me and asked me how I knew when he was bluffing. I really didn't know, because he wasn't the person that I was focusing on, so just for the heck of it, I told Joe that he "blushed" every time he tried bluffing. Now I really didn't mean that, I just made it up, but BELIEVE IT OR NOT, when we started playing again, every single time that Joe "bluffed," he began blushing.

I absolutely could not believe it!

NOW, I fully understand how POWERFUL the human mind can be. I actually planted a seed in Joe's mind and talked him into blushing whenever he bluffed.

I actually fooled myself!

Oh, I never did spot the person suspected of cheating, and I was REALLY glad about that.

Tip number two involves fidgeting. If you ask someone a question, and they begin to fidget, there is a good chance that the person is lying, especially if they are not normally fidgety.

In poker, if you are sitting across the table from a person who wasn't fidgeting, and all of a sudden they go ALL IN, and they start fidgeting around, there is a strong chance that they are bluffing.

The third tip is to listen for changes in the voice tone. If a person's voice all of a sudden goes up an octave, then there's a good chance they are excited, and their Glossopharyngeal nerve is kicking in.

The glossopharyngeal nerve is the 9th cranial nerve, I just thought I'd throw that in there!

The fourth thing that I watch for is the facial expressions. The 7th cranial nerve is the facial nerve, and it controls your expressions.

There is a "sure fire" way to effect a person's facial nerve, but I'm keeping that "top secret" for now!

This next series of tips, I like to call oculoreaction. (See Appendix D)

Your third cranial nerve is called your oculomotor nerve. That's why I like to call this section Oculoreaction. The oculomotor nerve controls pupil dilation in the iris. In most people, their pupils dilate when they get excited. Once again, you have to be very observant, have good eyesight or have powerful glasses like I do. That's why I like to wear my prescription sunglasses. They are very powerful and enable me to see better than 20/20 vision.

As far as I know, a person cannot stop themselves from having their pupils dilate.

Don't get me wrong. I'm not an ophthalmologist or a medical practitioner of any kind. I am just a very keen observer of human conduct and of emotional intelligence clues.

When the vast majority of poker players get cards and see pocket aces or pocket kings, I'm sure their eyes usually dilate. Most people's eyes will give away the fact that they are excited about the cards they hold. Some people may be able to control their outward excitement, but it is very difficult, if not impossible, to control your INNER self.

A great clue to watch for is a person's blink pattern. Many people will change their pattern after being asked a question. So if their blink pattern is normal, and after asking a question they all of a sudden start blinking more rapidly or they don't blink at all, then there is a good chance that the person is fibbing.

Some people may even look away after asking them a question, especially if you're looking them in the eyes. It may just be a very brief glance, so always be alert when watching for it.

These eye clues are another reason a lot of poker players probably wear sun glasses themselves, to prevent opponents from reading their eyes.

I have attached a list of the twelve cranial nerves in "Appendix E, so that you can also study the cranial nerves and use this them as a training aid.

Another form of study in learning to read people involves micro-expressions. A micro expression is a very brief involuntary facial expression or emotion being experienced at the time. These can usually be seen when a person is asked a question.

You have to be extremely on top of your game to follow these, because micro-expressions happen so briefly and quickly pass.

I am not going to get into a lot of detail here other than just to create awareness about micro expressions. There are several great books on the subject. As your experience in reading people grows and your emotional intelligence increases you can ultimately expand into the study of micro-expressions.

Like anything else, you want to walk before you can run. The best way to describe this is, if you want to learn physics, you must first learn algebra, trig and calculus. After mastering them, you would THEN move onto more complex formulas, etc.

That's exactly what we're doing here. You have to learn some basic stuff, master that and then you move on because that's how the brain works. It loves learning new things!

Let's back up here a little bit. I want to emphasize that all of the things I've been writing about here, like body language, reading eyes, tells, etc., take us back to a word you will see often in this book, (FOCUS). In order to detect these "messages" accurately you must always FOCUS. Developing focus is, in itself, an exercise of emotional intelligence.

If you are not focused you are not going to be successful in your search for clues left by the actions of the person(s) you are observing (with all of your senses). Focus, memory, and reading people, ALL go hand in hand.

Start with the five tips I gave you on how to read lies, then sit down and play some card games and practice reading your opponents. Then, take a walk in the mall or the park, and just observe people. Watch the different reactions.

When I am walking around in Times Square, I learn more in an hour or two about people, then I ever thought possible!

Another thing that I have recently began to study was taxi drivers. I've talked to so many cab drivers about reading their passengers that I can probably right a book on that alone.

You wouldn't believe how many taxi drivers take "reading people" so seriously.

From Los Angeles to New York, and almost every city across the country, even taxi drivers are working on their emotional intelligence.

I talked to a taxi driver in Washington DC once who knew all about emotional intelligence. He told me that he reads a person in a matter of seconds, and decides whether he should pick that person up or not. He actually went into detail of what he looks for, and in my opinion, he definitely knew what he was talking about.

Another cab driver in Las Vegas told me how much safer it was to drive a cab in Vegas, compared to NY and Boston. He also told me that he "reads people" before letting them in his cab, ever since he was held up at gun point in NY.

A New York City cab driver once told me that at least half of his fellow taxi driver friends in NY City had been robbed at least once in their career. He told me that reading people was his survival skill.

In London, England, taxi drivers REALLY take it to the extreme. Not only do they learn how to read people, but to become a cab driver, they have to pass the ultimate brainteaser known as "The Knowledge Test." To pass the test, they have to commit to memory more than 25,000 roads, streets, lanes, avenues, etc. In addition to that, they have to also learn another 20,000 landmarks.

Talk about exercising your brain!

The combination of learning how to read people, memory training and exercising your brain, makes a very powerful formula for advanced emotional intelligence.

Chapter 7

Memory

"I am an ordinary man who worked hard to develop the talent I was given." —Muhammad Ali

I have memorized massive amounts of information over the last 10 years. The memory feats that I've accomplished were all self-taught and have dramatically improved my life.

I offer two practical pieces of advice to people who I work with when helping them expand their knowledge base and memory bank.

First, do not be afraid to challenge yourself. The vast majority of people feel that studying is over when they finish formal schooling. This does not have to be the case.

You should NEVER want to stop learning. Virtually everyone, especially those with high emotional intelligence, are capable of learning well beyond their 70's. You are also capable of improving your memory far beyond what you thought possible!

Expand your mind. Never stop exercising your brain. Never stop growing.

The second piece of this advice is to study and understand the basic principles of study and adding to your base of knowledge. I know that sounds a bit confusing and repetitive. Let me clarify.

I did not memorize all of the countries of the world and their capitals in one brief sitting. I surely didn't commit to memory 80,000 U.S. zip codes in a day or two.

It took effort and hard work. Each success broadened the foundation and gave me confidence that I could take on even bigger challenges. YOU can do the same thing.

Treat it like you are erecting a tall building. First you build a very solid foundation. After the foundation is complete, you begin working on the main floor. Then you go to the next level and continue to add floors.

Unlike a building, the structure that YOU are building has no known limitations.

You are limited only by your own will, commitment and creativity.

Focus intently on what you are studying. Be present in the moment. Literally, feel yourself internalizing the material and making it a part of the core of your being. Follow that path of study with extreme focus, and your long-term memory will hold vast amounts of knowledge far beyond what you could have ever imagined.

One of the keys to MY memory success was the use of flashcards.

The first thing I actually wrote on flashcards was information from the World Almanac. I started by writing down and memorizing countries of the world and got up to about 200 or so countries. Countries like Uzbekistan and Kyrgyzstan, I couldn't even pronounce them or spell them back then.

I had a show scheduled in Philadelphia which is about a 4 to 5 hour drive from where I was living at the time. I took the flashcards with me and had almost every country in the world written down on these flashcards. During the five hour trip to Philadelphia I began reviewing the 200 countries. Then when I drove back the next day, I reviewed the countries again in my head and began remembering them. When I got home, I reviewed them one last time while on my exercise bike. In just two days, I memorized ALL 200 countries and never forgot them.

I then did the same thing with the capitals of the countries. In about a week, I had memorized EVERY country and capital in the world.

One day my daughter asked me to help her study the chemical elements on the Periodic Table.

I used the same process, by writing the chemical elements on flashcards, and within two days, my daughter had them memorized. The strange thing about it was, I actually failed chemistry back when I was in high school, because I never knew the chemical elements. After helping my daughter to memorize the elements, I TOO remembered all 111 chemical elements on the Periodic Table.

I discovered that the best way to memorize things for me, was while riding my exercise bike. I also enjoyed doing memory work while flying to a show. I always arrived at my destination feeling refreshed, like I had been meditating the whole time.

Let me give you an example of how I used the flashcards with the countries.

Each card had a number from 1 to 200 printed on one side. On the opposite side was the country. For example, number 1 was Israel, number 2 was Poland, number 3 was Canada, number 4 was Zimbabwe, etc... This would go all the way up to 200, which was Wales.

On a different set of flashcards, I would have the 111 chemical elements from the Periodic Table. On yet another set, I would have all the Oscar winners from 1928 until present. The flashcards were much easier to work with than words on a page or even a computer screen. They were also easier to work with while I was on the exercise bike.

When I first started doing my memory work, smart phones were not like they are today. My study patterns have evolved since the smart phones improved. I NOW create flashcards on my cell phone.

The memory work helped me pass HOURS on my exercise bike. The exercise bike was the perfect time and place to use the flashcards as a memory tool. It was a perfect combination. My body and my brain received hours of vigorous and healthy training at the same time. I still have thousands of the flashcards that I used over the years.

The United States Playing Card Company once sent me over a thousand decks of "blank faced" playing cards for throwing practice. I ended up using several thousand blank cards to make my flash cards.

The in-depth memory work started off as something to kill time on the bike. I had no idea at the time that it would lead to where I am today. I also discovered that people were really "digging" the memory stuff. After my college shows, I would challenge the students by asking them to name any country in the world, and if I didn't know the correct capital, they would win $100. I would then throw the World Almanac out to the audience and have them pick any country from the book, just to make it even more challenging.

Just like when I first learned magic, the expressions on the people's faces, were priceless. I love seeing people amazed. I love putting a smile on a person's face. I thrive on that reaction. That's what motivates ME! I found a new skill and it had nothing to do with magic whatsoever, yet it had the SAME impact on the crowd.

I was out to entertain my audience, the smiles, the thrills, the shocked look.

That's what I was trying to do, get a reaction.

When I first started learning the memory stuff, it wasn't about, "Hey, look what I've memorized." My motivation came from my audience's reaction, and it made me want to learn more and more.

Motivation and memory go hand in hand.

At the same time I was learning more, I was exercising my brain. It motivated me to get on the bike more, which ended up being healthier as well. There were also psychological benefits for me. I barely made it out of high school. I had to go to summer school to graduate. I only attended community college for a few years and never graduated.

Suddenly, I had reason to be proud of my intellectual accomplishments.

My memory study fed my emotional intelligence, and my greater emotional intelligence spurred on my memory practices. I spent hours on the bike due to my heart condition. I was bored, and the memory work kept me FOCUSED – I love that word.

In the process, my heart issue went away. I became far more confident in myself and rippled over with newfound feelings of higher self-esteem. I began to look forward, and still do, to long sessions on the exercise bike because of all the things I was learning.

It was an incredibly productive wheel of connection. Healthier body. Healthier mind. Skyrocketing self-esteem. More material to excite and entertain my audiences. The joy of learning. Embracing and understanding the meaning of emotional intelligence. And to think it all began with making a few flash cards of countries to keep from being bored on my exercise bike.

After memorizing all the ZIP Codes in the U.S., I decided to utilize them in my show as well. I was at the United States Military Academy performing and ALL the states in the country are represented there. A cadet would stand up and say "90027, Sir." I would say "You're from Los Angeles." Another cadet would say,"99923," and I would say, "Alaska, you're from Alaska." The cadets absolutely loved it!

I really loved to engage my crowds, and I would always do something that added a personal touch.

One day a friend of mine known as the "Human Calculator," did this routine where he asked me my birth date, then immediately told me the day of the week that it fell on. Once again, I just had to learn how to do that.

Although I wasn't a human calculator like Scott, I did, however, have a way to pull it off. I looked up the dates on the computer, and memorized every day of the week for every date, all the way back to 1953.

When a few senior citizens came up to me at an event and asked me what day of the week THEY were born, I decided to memorize the dates all the way back to 1925.

Believe it or not, after a few months of studying, I can now tell you the day of the week for EVERY SINGLE DATE, all the way back to 1AD!

The passion of being able to do something personal is what drove me to memorize all those dates. It doesn't get any more entertaining than to touch someone's personal life by knowing their birth date, ZIP code, or by knowing the city where they were born. That personal stuff connects BIGGER than any magic trick that I've discovered and knowing that kept me inspired.

I was on my way and could never look back. I thought, I'm doing something now that no performer has ever done. I was really doing something that you CAN'T BUY. I began looking at memory as a performance tool. That was how I started putting it into my performances.

In the last 6 months, things have changed significantly. I look at memory study not only as a performance piece but as a health practice. I look for every opportunity to share what I have discovered, because it can actually help people in so many ways.

I also began concentrating on remembering names and peoples' faces. This was not only important to me as a person and as a performer, but I found it was something that virtually everyone asked me how I could help them improve.

I wanted to be helpful and developed a few simple steps as a starting point.

Really stay focused when meeting someone.

Really make a positive effort to remember a person's name, immediately after they tell you it.

Always ask for a business card. Then be sure to glance at their name on the card to reinforce it in your mind.

Repeat their name silently in your head a few times after shaking their hand.

Look for an outstanding feature on the person's face or upper body. Like Jay Leno's chin, Michael Strahan's teeth, etc. I like to mentally associate objects or locations to people's names.

George (the state GEORGIA)
Wendy (visualize a tornado or a hamburger)
Rich (two $$ in his eyes)

Test. Experiment. Practice. Use whatever works best for YOU!

Think of something outrageous or crazy about the person or their occupation. The more extreme the image, the more likely you are to remember it.

FOCUS, FOCUS, FOCUS!

After meeting someone, as they are about to leave, repeat their name AGAIN by saying, "Nice meeting you, Debra." This will reinforce their name even further in your memory.

I didn't know about emotional intelligence back when I first began doing the exercise bike and the memory training. I knew something was happening though, I knew that the more I would get on my bike, and the more I would force-feed my brain to memorize things, there was something going on. I felt energy. I felt energetic. I felt more intuitive. I felt my brain was expanding. It was a weird sensation, but the best thing of all was the increased energy.

There was a change, not only physically but mentally. It was energizing me and charging me up and making me feel younger mentally, and physically. I felt really, really good. It's as if I tapped into the FOUNTAIN OF MENTAL YOUTH!

It was a combination of the physical and mental exercise.

It's bizarre what your mind is capable of. People are amazed when I tell them that I was in my 50s when I started doing this. It started sinking in, and I became more excited and began to grasp what it could all mean. I didn't really get into it heavily until I was 60 years old, after it was confirmed that my health issue was mysteriously gone.

The exercise and feeding the brain worked together with the bike riding to produce a whole new me! I was far more physically and mentally fit then I had ever been in MY ENTIRE LIFE.

I wanted to know MORE. I wanted specifics and details in the fields I was studying.

I wanted to know about the physiology of how the brain worked.

A great friend I met while working at Walter Reed Medical Center, Dr. Neil Grunberg, encouraged me to include cranial nerves and emotional intelligence with my memory work. THAT was the very first time that I ever heard of Emotional Intelligence.

I took Dr. Neil's advice to heart, but I feel that he may have created a monster!

I am NOW studying and learning about the human brain at a pace that far exceeds even MY expectations.

I have found it enormously helpful and exhilarating to learn how the brain functions. I am now only beginning to understand exactly what is going on with ME.

I have come to know that our minds can embrace a concept and both hold and exude enthusiasm for that concept, far better when you can visualize, with specificity, how it all works.

Knowledge is DEFINITELY power! The more specific the knowledge, the greater the power. And it ALL begins with MEMORY and FOCUS!

It is still really funny to me. People come up and say, you must have a photographic memory. You must be a savant. You are a genius. You must have made straight A's.

Are you kidding me?

I'm a steelworker with no college degree who got laid off and started doing magic tricks to feed my family.

I'm as ordinary and regular a guy as you will ever find.

You may not want to take memory work to the extremes like I have, but you will be amazed at what you can do if you make up your mind to just do it.

I like to use the analogy of the Rocky movie. In the original Rocky when he found that he was going to fight Apollo Creed, he gets up in the morning, he drinks his glass of eggs and goes outside and starts trying to jog. In a couple of blocks he's getting side stickers and can't even go on.

Right before his fight, however, after weeks and months of training he's running to the top of the steps of the Art Museum, jumping up and down. That's the way your brain works. You start off slow and you keep at it. You keep feeding it more and more stuff and seemingly all of a sudden, BAM, you become a "super brain." You realize that your brain works just like the muscles in your body.

Rest is, also, just as important for your brain as it is for your body. Weightlifters, runners and athletes of all types know how important it is to rest your body. When you work out, one of the most important things is to let your body rest and relax your muscles. It is the same with the brain. Don't neglect that part of the process. Get adequate sleep. Rest when your body and brain are telling you it is needed. Meditate. These are all important parts of keeping a brain functioning at a high level.

It's amazing what's been happening and how all these doctors have become a part of my life, all these neuroscientists, neurobiologists, neuropsychologists and others. Some of them even want to study me! They want to find out if what I am doing can be used to treat people with Alzheimer's and dementia. I have become more inspired to see how far I can go and grow, so that I can help others!

I have accelerated my study of the brain. I just keep reading and absorbing knowledge. I probably have absorbed more knowledge in the last three months than I did in the first 62 years of my life. I expect the same will be true of the next three months!

Let me say again, I'm not a doctor. I don't have a PhD, but I am doing a heck of a lot of research now, because I want to know what's going on.

How is it that a 62-year-old guy could absorb all of this knowledge and retain it in his long-term memory? What is causing this?

All I have learned about the brain has been an amazing discovery for me. I want to push my brain as far as I can push it because your long-term memory has an unlimited capacity.

It's like the universe, just like the billions and billions of stars in the universe. That's what your brain is like, with the billions and billions of neurons.

With neurotransmitters firing off constantly. I never realized, and very few people have a clue, about all the things that take place in the brain to create a memory. How many neurons are put into effect just to do a simple thing, it's just amazing.

The more I learn and the more knowledge I absorb, the more I want to learn. I am going to study until the day I die. I just love it and wish everybody could experience this.

If I didn't know better I would swear my brain stopped aging, and is becoming younger. I feel like I have the brain of a 25 year old again. My brain is just so active it's so alert, and I have total control over it.

My latest example of having control over my brain and memory, JUST happened as I was about to finish this book. I had all of the chapters finished, and I was working on the Appendix. I actually kept this entire book on my cell phone. I had not given all my latest edits to Dale Ledbetter.

All of a sudden, I pressed something on my phone and the ENTIRE BOOK was DELETED. I was devastated. The latest changes I had made were completely erased. What happened next was absolutely UNBELIEVABLE.

I sat on my couch where I usually memitate, and started writing from the beginning. As I was writing, I began to remember (WORD FOR WORD), every single paragraph in each chapter. It was absolutely amazing! The final version of the book that you are reading now, was written from memory. That's what high emotional intelligence is all about!

Focus, memory, bouncing back from adversity, overcoming obstacles, staying positive, and maintaining self-control. Incredible!!!

Getting back to MEMORY. I truly believe that almost ANYONE can learn how to improve their memory and brain function. If you have the passion and desire to really improve, then you can. Like I said before, you have to be willing to put some time into it. I began with 30 to 45 minutes a day and the results were phenomenal. You can put as little or as much time as you want into the process. Decide what you want to learn, what areas you want to master and then – just do it.

I promise that you will amaze yourself. Then YOU will become an inspiration for others as YOU begin to amaze them.

BUT DON'T FORGET!

To maintain proper focus and cognitive fitness you must get proper rest. You must balance the study and challenges you impose on your brain with the amount of rest the brain needs to accomplish the tasks presented to it.

Here is a great start. It is a memory technique that I developed and, have personally used myself. I have also found it effective in training others. I have taught this system at middle schools, high schools, Walter Reed, Fort Belvoir and Florida Hospital.

If you can memorize these 10 celebrities in numerical order from 1 to 10, you will be on your way to building YOUR OWN Mental Matrix.

Here is a celebrity list and some tips to remember them to the number:

1. Denzel Washington

   (Just visualize George Washington, the FIRST President, crossing the Delaware, then you will remember that Denzel Washington is ALSO #1)

2. Brad Pitt

   (B For Brad, 2nd letter in the alphabet, two T's in Pitt)

3. Tom Cruise

   (3 letters in "Tom", or "C" in Cruise, third letter of the alphabet)

4. George Clooney

   (Four, George, sort of rhymes)

5. Michael J. Fox

   (Fox Five or FOX 5 News)

6. Chris Rock

   (Six, Chris, try your best here) Sometimes, the harder ones are the easiest to remember

7. Sylvester Stallone

   (Sylvester Stallone, seven ALL begin with "S")

8. Tiger Woods

   (I think of an "Eight Iron" in golf)

9. Nick Nolte

   (Nine, Nick, Nolte, all begin with the letter "N")

10. Vince Vaughn

    (The letter "V" in roman numerals equals "5". So "V" plus "V" equals "10".

Once you put these celebrities to memory, watch how easy it becomes to learn other things by associating them to the celebrities.

Here are the first TEN states admitted in to the union:

1. Delaware

    (If you remember Denzel Washington as number "1" you will remember Washington crossing the Delaware)

2. Pennsylvania

    (If you remember Brad Pitt as number "2" just think of PITT as in Pittsburgh, and you will remember Pennsylvania)

3. New Jersey

    (Think of Tom Cruise, cruising the NJ coast in a big yacht)

4. Georgia

    (George, Georgia,)

5. Connecticut

    (If you remember Michael J. Fox, Fox reminds ME of Foxwoods casino, which is in Connecticut)

6. Massachusetts

    (Chris Rock, Plymouth Rock)

7. Maryland

    (Sylvester Stallone always needed a doctor in his Rocky movies, (MD) another name for doctor and for Maryland)

8. South Carolina

   (Tiger Woods playing golf on some of the nation's most beautiful golf courses in Myrtle Beach, SC)

9. New Hampshire

   (Nick Nolte New Hampshire)

10. Virginia

   (Vince Vaughn Virginia)

If you want to go further, the 11th state in the union is New York. Just remember Sept 11th, or the two towers looking like the number 11. Amazing!

You are more likely to remember something if you speak out loud instead of just reading it silently to yourself.

These are just a few specifics on how to increase the effectiveness of particular neurotransmitters. Let me summarize by offering five general tips that may be beneficial to you in increasing your levels of all the neurotransmitters we have discussed:

1. **Positive Thinking and Happiness.**

2. **Exercising daily, both physically AND mentally.**

3. **Good Nutrition.**

4. **Listening to your favorite music, especially when exercising.**

5. **Drink coffee or tea.**

The Human Brain has 100 Billion neurons, each neuron is connected to 10,000 other neurons, just think about that a second.

Chapter 8

Sex, "Neurotransmitters" and Rock N' Roll

"I think music in itself is healing. It's an explosive expression of humanity. It's something we are all touched by. No matter what culture we're from, EVERYONE LOVES MUSIC." —Billy Joel

Neurotransmitters are brain chemicals that relay signals between nerve cells, called "neurons." Neurotransmitters are capable of turning our life into an exciting world, if we can learn how to utilize them correctly.

Neurotransmitters and emotional intelligence go hand in hand. I have spent many hours learning the relationship between particular neurotransmitters and specific physical or emotional actions.

Through daily exercise, both physical and mental, we all have the power to make ourselves happier and healthier.

In the last 20 years, people have become less dependent on their MINDS and have also become less active physically. Society has become more prone to stress, depression and anxiety. Taking a pill has become the "quick fix" to all our problems.

I have found that by making some simple lifestyle changes, ANYONE can improve their brain health and memory. The results will make you feel better and will inspire you to achieve your highest human potential. Neurotransmitters play a key role in making this possible. They are critically important and play many roles in determining our individuality.

Understanding what takes place in the brain every time a thought or an action is initiated and completed will help you realize the control that YOU can exert over that process.

This all begins with the neurons which are the cells in your brain that process messages. There are approximately 100 billion neurons in the human brain.

Neurons communicate with one another using axons. When a message arrives at a synapse the neurotransmitter is released which signals the receiving neuron as to what action it should take. Neurons need still more help which comes from glial cells. There are 50 glial cells for every one neuron cell. These glial cells are critical because they maintain the required balance of all of the chemicals that populate the brain.

I find that by understanding this process, I can directly influence it through thoughts. It is one thing to visualize or direct your thoughts to accomplish a task. It is far more likely to be successful if you can emotionalize the "feeling" by knowing exactly what you are directing the thought to do and what has to happen inside your brain to produce the desired effect. Imagine the power of choice and direction that this gives you.

The power in this choice is the very essence of emotional intelligence.

Let's go back to the specific role of neurotransmitters. Neurotransmitters are natural chemicals inside our body that transmit messages between our nerve cells (neurons). As mentioned, these chemicals allow the "neurons" to communicate messages by transmitting signals from one neuron to another across a "junction" known as a SYNAPSE. Without neurotransmitters, our neurons would not be able to communicate with each other.

Neurotransmitters help control our vital organs, from our heart and lungs to our stomach. They also affect our memory, mood, sleep, and much, much more.

One of the more interesting things that neurotransmitters control is SEX DRIVE. You can actually improve your sex life by boosting a few key neurotransmitters.

Neurotransmitters like Dopamine, GABA, Acetylcholine, Oxytocin, and Nitric Oxide, can all improve libido.

DOPAMINE heightens sex drive and pleasure.
ACETYLCHOLINE is known to improve arousal.
SEROTONIN improves mood and intimacy.
GABA relaxes you, enhances concentration.
OXYTOCIN is known as the LOVE hormone.
NITRIC OXIDE opens blood vessels, which is
essential to a great sex life!

Through things like proper nutrition, daily exercise and positive thought, we can enhance these specific neurotransmitters. Even meditation has been known to boost neurotransmitters. Eating dark chocolate and bananas are two of MY favorite ways to raise neurotransmitter levels.

Studies also show, that DOPAMINE and other neurotransmitters, can be greatly enhanced by listening to your favorite music. The more PLEASING the music, the more pleasurable the experience can become!

I can definitely assure you, that this is true!

The natural high and euphoric feelings that I experience when listening to Aerosmith, Guns N' Roses, Nirvana and Led Zeppelin while lifting weights, is INDESCRIBABLE. I have found that the more I push my brain, PRIOR to working out, the more

AMAZING the feelings become during the weight lifting workout. The feelings enhance greatly when turning up the music.

These feelings are caused by our neurotransmitters. The combination of working out my brain and body at the same time, then lifting weights right afterwards, has worked wonders for me.

Unlike drugs, neurotransmitters are safe and NATURAL!

Neurotransmitters can also cause negative symptoms as well, especially when they are out of whack. Low levels of some neurotransmitters can cause many diseases and illnesses. It is very important to identify the neurotransmitters that need the boost, so that you do not make your imbalance worse.

Alcohol, drugs, poor diet and poor mental attitude, are just some of the things that can deplete our neurotransmitter levels.

There are more than 50 known neurotransmitters. Here are some of the more important ones and what they do, so that you can take the right actions to try to optimize your balance appropriately:

GABA (gamma aminobutyric acid)

GABA is an inhibitory neurotransmitter that slows down the firing of neurons, creating a calming effect on our brain and body.

GABA affects our brain similar to the way Valium does. It reduces anxiety and stress.

Studies show that you can increase GABA naturally by practicing yoga or doing meditation.

Studies have also shown that natural GABA can be found in some teas and cherry tomatoes.

I have found that challenging my memory every day, not only exercises my brain, but it also increases GABA. I call this practice "MEMITATION", (See Appendix D) which is my own form of meditation. I usually "memitate" for at least an hour a day in a nice, quiet setting.

Acetylcholine

Acetylcholine helps stimulate muscles and is associated with learning and MEMORY.

Lifting weights or doing any type of resistance exercise can help increase acetylcholine levels in our body.

Recent studies have found that EXERCISING your BRAIN regularly, not only helps increase acetylcholine levels, but may also delay the onset of Alzheimer's disease. Alzheimer's patients are shown to have low levels of Acetylcholine.

Serotonin

Serotonin has an amazing effect on emotion, mood and anxiety. Higher serotonin levels help boost self-esteem!

Studies show that significantly low levels of serotonin may be associated with depression.

Studies also show that POSITIVE THOUGHT and POSITIVE ATTITUDE help naturally raise the level of serotonin in our body.

Exercising the body AND mind regularly is very important for serotonin as for virtually every other mental or physical function of our body.

Good nutrition, like fruits and vegetables, including my favorites, milk and bananas, may help increase serotonin levels.

Dopamine

Dopamine regulates the PLEASURABLE emotions in the brain and body. Studies have shown that dopamine enhances motivation and focus.

Parkinson's disease is associated with a significant LOW LEVEL of dopamine.

Positive attitude, enjoyable activities and daily exercise, all produce MORE dopamine, as do eating dark chocolate and bananas.

Laughter and just "plain old fun," can also help produce more dopamine.

Anandamide

Anandamide is the neurotransmitter of extreme pleasure. Some call it the brain's own MARIJUANA!

Anandamide is very similar to "tetrahydrocannabinol," (THC) better known as "cannabis."

It also plays an important role in memory and pain.

Anandamide can be found in dark chocolate and cocoa. Two MORE of my favorites!

Nitric Oxide

In my opinion, the most interesting neurotransmitter to our health is Nitric Oxide.

It may well be the secret weapon of neurotransmitters. It causes our blood vessels to dilate, preventing the formation of clots, while promoting better circulation and regulating blood pressure.

Nitric Oxide can also increase the levels of oxygen in our body, which can help things like memory, sleep, endurance, strength, etc.

Weight lifting and running are great ways to release nitric oxide in our bodies. Things like nuts, dairy and certain fruits, can help increase nitric oxide.

Oxytocin

Oxytocin is known as the "love" molecule.

If you hug somebody, you are BOTH increasing your oxytocin.

Studies show that watching an emotionally compelling movie, like "RUDY" or "ROCKY," may also make your oxytocin levels increase.

Believe it or not, petting or cuddling with your dog increases your oxytocin levels. Your dog may also receive the same benefit!

Epinephrine

Epinephrine is a hormone and a neurotransmitter that is also known as "ADRENALINE."

Strong emotions like fear and anger, cause epinephrine to be released in the bloodstream.

This reaction is known as the "Flight or Fight" response and creates a surge of energy when released.

The "Epipen" is a like a shot of epinephrine, which is used in the treatment of allergic reactions.

Melatonin

Melatonin is both a hormone and a neurotransmitter that controls our sleep cycle. Melatonin is also associated with mood and sexual behavior.

Studies show that bananas, tomatoes and rice may help increase our levels of melatonin.

Endorphins

Endorphins are our body's way of blocking pain and promoting calmness.

Endorphins can affect us like codeine and other pain medication does, by giving us a euphoric feeling, but without the addiction.

Intense physical training can produce large amounts of endorphins.

Dark chocolate and bananas are known to "naturally" boost your endorphins.

I have been able to achieve these "euphoric highs," occasionally during my weight lifting sessions.

Adenosine

Adenosine makes you tired and drowsy and promotes sleep.

Adenosine is also good for the heart, because it dilates the blood vessels and improves circulation.

There are more than 50 known additional neurotransmitters.

I threw this discussion in on important neurotransmitters, because of the similarity between the chemicals in our body and emotional intelligence. They impact each other in so many ways.

Understanding that process can be a big help in learning how your thoughts and lifestyle can control the performance of those neurotransmitters.

Caffeine and Neurotransmitters

Caffeine gets a lot of negative publicity. Recent studies however, show that drinking coffee may actually be good for you!

Within a few minutes after you drink a cup of coffee or tea, caffeine is carried by your bloodstream to all of your organs and every cell in your body.

It is quickly and completely absorbed from the stomach and intestines into the blood stream. Caffeine also passes through the blood-brain barrier very easily.

Studies have also shown that caffeine may affect some of our major neurotransmitters in a POSITIVE way, including dopamine and acetylcholine.

The transmission of caffeine improves our mood, and some doctors I have spoken with think it may protect brain cells from age and disease related degeneration. Increasing caffeine improves muscular activity and may also improve long-term memory.

This coffee thing has really got my attention, especially since I always drink coffee when I'm on the road performing, and I have two or three cups of tea each day when I'm at home. Drinking coffee and tea, in my opinion, and based on my experience, impacts a host of the body's neurotransmitters and research shows that it may enable us to tap into our hidden potential in three major areas:

Cognitive skills:

May sharpen reasoning, memory, concentration, and decision-making and heightens sensory perception.

Affective:

Enhances moods, increases relaxation, relieves boredom, and boosts self-confidence.

Physical:

Improves speed, endurance, energy output, strength, and reaction time, and may increase thermogenesis, that is, fat burning and metabolic rate.

These are just a few specifics on how to increase the effectiveness of particular neurotransmitters. Let me summarize by offering five general tips that may be beneficial to you in increasing your levels of all the neurotransmitters we have discussed:

1. **Positive Thinking and Happiness.**
2. **Exercising daily, both physically AND mentally.**
3. **Good Nutrition.**
4. **Listening to your favorite music, especially when exercising.**
5. **Drink coffee or tea.**

Chapter 9

Cognitive Fitness

"Physical fitness is not only one of the most important keys to a healthy body, it is the basis of dynamic and creative intellectual activity." —John F. Kennedy

COGNITIVE fitness is just as important as PHYSICAL fitness when it comes to health, wellness and emotional intelligence. Daily mental exercise allows the brain to grow, promoting healthy brain performance. It is your most powerful tool in the battle against memory loss and the savages of dementia.

If a weightlifter only worked his arms, he would look strange and be ineffective in his sport. The same is true with brain exercises and memory training.

Effective cognitive fitness is a combination of memory work, emotional intelligence training, focus and all aspects of improving your brain functions. To maximize results you must approach this process, not as isolated exercises, but as a comprehensive package of techniques.

After I became immersed in memory training and spending more and more time doing it, I realized there were collateral benefits.

I knew I was onto something. It was no longer just about performance. It was more than just brain exercise. Brain exercise became cognitive fitness!

The idea of cognitive fitness came into play before knowing about the collateral benefits of memory enhancement. I didn't know it at the time. I was just doing memory work to kill time on the bike, and then all of a sudden I was doing it more and becoming more inspired because I was seeing that it was impressing people and entertaining people.

I realized the combination of physical and brain exercise was helping me physically and mentally. I then started throwing around the term, cognitive fitness. A new kind of fitness, I felt like I invented it. The way I was doing it was very unique. The way I was force-feeding my brain and memorizing extensive things was energizing every aspect of my being.

I would be on my bike memorizing, "Four score and seven years ago our fathers brought forth on this continent, a new nation..."

I was going into every possible subject you could imagine from math, to science, to astronomy, geography, history, chemistry, subjects that I never did well in school. I never identified the chemical elements of the periodic table. I failed chemistry when I was in high school. Now, after a short period of intense focus, I knew every chemical element.

It was an embodiment of cognitive fitness.

I exercise my brain like an NFL or Olympic athlete works out their body. The term "use it or lose it" applies to your brain and memory skills, just as much as it does to your physical skills. The more you work out your brain, the healthier and stronger it will become. Whether you are 5 years old or 85 years old exercising your brain every day will make you more cognitively FIT. (cogfit)

We have all heard the saying that laughter is the best medicine. This definitely holds true for the brain and memory. Laughter not only engages multiple regions of the brain, but it reduces stress and helps increase emotional intelligence.

Laughter is the best medicine and stress is the polar opposite. Stress is the brain's worst enemy. It destroys brain cells and damages the hippocampus, where our memory is known to originate.

Watching a good comedian like Kevin Hart or a funny Jim Carrey movie can work wonders.

Studies show that different types of meditation can help improve the conditions of anxiety, depression, chronic pain, diabetes and high blood pressure. It can also improve focus, memory, creativity and learning skills. All are key ingredients for higher emotional intelligence. The best-known versions of meditation are guided mindfulness and transcendental meditation (TM). A third type of meditation is gaining popularity and is effective. It is called primordial sound meditation (PSM). It involves listening to sounds that are designed to lower the speed of your brain waves.

All these forms of meditation have proven to be highly effective at putting the mind into a relaxed state.

I have my own form of meditation that I call "MEMI-TATION." I usually sit on my couch and relax as I review things in my mind that I have already memorized. It is SO relaxing as well as beneficial for my memory. Memitation has changed my life dramatically. Using memitation has allowed me to take quantum leaps in mastering complex material that would have stumped me in the past.

Memitation has had a physical impact on my brain. The thickness of my cerebral cortex has increased. Memitating also encourages more connections between brain cells, all of which increases mental sharpness and memory ability. Memitation is a fantastic way to exercise your brain.

The "absolute key" to exercising your brain is to make it challenging and enjoyable at the same time. It is also very important to learn new things. Your brain becomes accustomed very quickly. Once you become very good at something, move on to something "new." This is the key to keeping your neurons firing.

Here are some great tips for using cognitive fitness to heighten your emotional intelligence:

Pay Attention

You will never remember anything, if you never first learned it. This is another way of saying one of my favorite words again – FOCUS. It is very important to pay attention and be a good listener.

Build Up Your Own Mental Matrix

As you learn additional or new information, you have to associate it and connect it to the existing knowledge and information that you already know.

Rehearse and Review

REPEAT, REPEAT, REPEAT. I constantly practice repeating during "memitation." This has been a FANTASTIC brain exercise for me. Memitation is the ultimate cognitive fitness exercise.

Visualization

Try visualizing specific things that you want to memorize or things that you want to achieve. Get "inside" those visualizations. I like to create funny and outrageous situations. They seem to stick better because there is a greater emotional attachment.

Read

Reading is a great brain exercise, especially reading challenging things like facts, figures or research. I really love reading and researching every night about the brain.

Focus on what you are doing on the computer. Make every task you take on a research project. Looking up words that you don't know the meaning of is extremely important. I try learning at least one new word every day.

Scrabble, Trivial Pursuit and Other Board Games

Playing these games has been a great boost to my cognitive fitness. They also add a social ingredient that is very important. I once memorized every question and answer in a trivial pursuit game just to mess with people. A great SCRABBLE tip, is to learn all the two letter words:

AA, AB, AD, AE, AG, AH, AI, AL, AM, AN, AR, AS, AT, AW, AX, AY, BA, BE, BI, BO, BY, DE, DO, ED, EF, EH, EL, EM, EN, ER, ES, ET, EX, FA, GO, HA, HE, HI, HO, HM, ID, IF, IN, IS, IT, JO, KA, LA, LI, LO, MA, ME, MI, MO, MU, MY, MM, NA, NE, NO, NU, OD, OE, OF, OH, OM, ON, OP, OR, OS, OW, OX,

OY, PA, PE, PI, RE, SH, SI, SO, TA, TI, TO, UH, UM, UN, UP, US, UT, WR, WO, XI, XU, YA, YE, YO, FE, ZA, QI, KI, OI.

Poker

Playing poker is not only a great mental exercise, but it also helps reduce stress.

Poker, as examined in more detail in this book, is also a great way to increase emotional intelligence.

Chess and Checkers

These are both very tactical, and incredibly strategic, games which makes them great workouts for the brain, and, as mentioned before, a great way to improve Focus!

Video Games

Video games are not only a good brain exercise, they may also help you become a better and more creative problem solver. Today's video games can now even guide you through a good cardio workout as well.

Begin a New Hobby

Magic is an excellent hobby. It not only exercises the brain, but also raises your emotional intelligence. I will be coming out with several new magic books and products very soon.

Knitting has done wonders for thousands of mothers and grandmothers.

Painting and drawing are fantastic exercises. Drawing was always my favorite hobby.

Any hobby that gets you learning NEW things is great for firing up those neurons in your brain.

These are 10 GREAT cognitive fitness tips. Use your imagination to create others.

What I'm about to show you NOW, is one of my favorite cognitive fitness exercises.

This alone can increase your emotional intelligence and lead to enhanced cognitive fitness:

Neuron Booster

THE STORY:

A deck of cards contains 52 cards, exactly the same amount of weeks in a year.

A deck of cards has four suits, and there are also four seasons.

A deck of cards has twelve court cards, (4 jacks, 4 queens and 4 kings), and there are also twelve months in a year.

Lastly, if you add up ALL of the spots (values) in a deck of cards, it totals 365, the same number of days in a year (this is if you count the jacks as 11, the queens as 12, the kings as 13 and aces as 1, and the Joker equals 1). If you add the other joker, you get 366. (Leap year)

THE EXERCISE:

Instead of adding ALL 364 spots, we are going to take a short cut using "2" steps.

Step 1: Each card is given a value:

Aces = 1

Jacks, queens, kings = 10

All the other values stay the same, 2=2, 3=3, 7=7, etc.

Step 2: Begin by placing one of the cards "faced down". Next you are going to look through the deck, one at a time, and you are going to maintain a count, but only focusing on the "single" digits.

Example:

If the first three cards are a 7, 5 and 3. The total is "15", but we are going to drop off the "1" in the number "15" and remember only the number "5."

So as we are counting, we are only going to keep a "single digit" count in our head.

* IMPORTANT to remember: (All "10" cards, which include tens, jacks, queens and kings will NOW be equal to "0")

Here is an example:

The first "six" cards are (7, 5, 3, 6, 2, 2). The total is "25," but your SINGLE DIGIT count is "5." If the next card is a "K," the count would still be at "5" because "K" is equal to "0."

If the next card is a "4", it would put your total at "9", if the next card is a "3", your count would be "2" instead of "12.'"

You continue this count until you get to the very last card! Whatever the ongoing total is at the end, all you have do is subtract that total from "10," and THAT will be the faced down card!

Example: If your total after adding all of the cards was 3, then (10 – 3 = 7) That would mean that the faced down card would be a "7."

This all works because of the 364 spot theory!

This is probably the absolute best brain exercise that you can ever do. It will help you boost your focus, memory, concentration and self-esteem, ALL of which are major components of higher emotional intelligence. It will also sharpen your math skills!

Most importantly, it will strengthen your brain and fire up your neurons, because there are over a trillion combinations with 52 cards. So every time you do it, your brain perceives NEW and challenging material, which helps promote brain growth!

This routine is also going to absolutely BLOW EVERYONE'S MIND! Your friends are going to think you're a "Card Counter." And in a way, you are!

Use my tips and ideas as a starting point. Stay focused. Experiment. You will soon develop your own list of effective cognitive fitness training methods.

Chapter 10

The Conscious and Subconscious Mind

"No problem can be solved from the same level of consciousness that created it." —*Albert Einstein*

People with heightened emotional intelligence usually have good communication skills between their own conscious mind and their subconscious mind.

What does that really mean?

To fully grasp the importance of the concept we need to first understand the functions of the conscious and the subconscious mind. Let's begin with basic definitions and functions:

Conscious mind – thinks, takes input from all your senses, learns and interprets that information and acts. (Voluntary thoughts and actions)

Subconscious mind – performs overlearned skills and is a reservoir for all thoughts, memories and habitual actions. (Involuntary thoughts and actions)

The single most important characteristic of a successful person is positive belief.

Positive belief is an essential ingredient for the person with heightened emotional intelligence. Since our thoughts may have the power to determine our reality, why would you not want to keep them POSITIVE?

The largest barrier to achieving positive belief is overcoming all of the negative programming embedded into the subconscious mind over the years.

We all have a voice that seems to sit on our shoulder all day and whisper in our ear. Sadly, most of the messages it sends us are negative, not positive. We have stressed throughout this book that, as human beings, we have choices.

One of the most important choices we have to make (or I should say that we are privileged to make) is to decide whether YOU are the whispering voice or whether you are the listening ear.

Enhanced emotional intelligence will help you make the decision to be the listening ear. You can choose to turn the voice off, to ignore it, or to demand that the message be changed from what is bad for you to what is good for you.

This is not an impossible task. It does require FOCUS, and it does require practice.

Monitor yourself throughout the day. You will make progress. Then you will lose ground. The voice will gain the upper hand. But, if you listen with all your senses and FEEL your reactions, you can recognize what is happening and put your own ship back on course.

If you let that voice go unchallenged it builds a library in your subconscious mind. That reservoir of thoughts, feelings and emotions can sabotage your plans, your goals your success and your happiness.

That does not have to be the case. Be the ear, not the voice.

Once you discipline the ear to filter what it allows into the inner sanctum of your brain you have taken a giant step toward heightened emotional intelligence. This level of AWARENESS allows you to get to know yourself and to take the actions that are critical to your emotional well-being.

Let's look at a few ways in which that is true.

Find Your Strengths

Be driven by the idea that you will never again have to think about the demeaning and ego deflating process of correcting your weaknesses. Search for those strengths, with the vigor of a captive seeking freedom, because that is what you will find – Freedom. Make the search to find your strengths a matter of serious FOCUS.

You will find freedom to be the real you. You'll find the joy of being able to excel. You will find the power of heightened emotional intelligence. Then, you only have to let go of the past, without a backward glance and race headlong into the inviting future.

Exploit Your Strengths

The combination of focus and awareness gives you the ability to exploit your strengths and to ignore your weaknesses. This is just one of the dominant character-istics of individuals with high emotional intelligence.

They constantly focus on their strengths and inten-tionally ignore their weaknesses. Some people who care about us may give bad advice in this regard. Family members, counselors, and friends sometimes advise us to work on improving weaknesses. This allows our strengths to diminish, and we end up frustrated, with lower self-esteem and become unhappy.

We end up wallowing in the misery caused by our own failures to correct weaknesses instead of reveling in the joys of success brought about by emphasizing our strengths.

If you know what your strengths are and you are not exploiting them (or it), then reverse course and seek that light of freedom and joy. If you don't know what your strengths are, then take charge. Become obsessed with seeking them out.

These are just a few suggestions. Make up your own list. Seek opinions from friends, teachers, colleagues or relatives as to what they think your strengths are. DON'T be dissuaded by any discouraging input you get. Listen, with all your senses to your internal thoughts and FEELINGS.

Love Yourself

There is no better way to love yourself then to set out to discover your strengths and then to have the courage to follow whereever that path leads. You will hit bumps. You will follow dead ends. Don't despair. Dig deep into your growing reservoir of emotional intelligence and the answer will seek you out.

Look Inside Yourself

Far too many people look outside themselves to find relief, direction or guidance.

They seldom find the path they are seeking. Ultimately, those who look inside themselves find emotional intelligence. They then nurture and control the choices in their lives. They heighten their emotional intelligence and achieve levels of success they never imagined for themselves. I am a living example of the truth of that statement!

Here is a simple and important tip for improving the content of your subconscious mind. You don't have to change every word in your vocabulary to bring about immense change. Just exchange one word for another and then buckle your seat belt. Change "but" to "and."

Every time you face a challenge, a decision or choice, make that change.

"I would really like to change jobs, but I'm not sure I can handle the new duties." Instead, say, "I would really like to change jobs, and I'm excited about the new challenges which will allow me to exploit my strengths."

"I would really like to move to a new city, but I would miss my friends." Instead say, "I would really like to move to a new city, and meeting new friends and having new experiences will be exciting."

This simple change will work wonders. Try it.

You can search the wisdom of the ages, and you will see repeatedly a key discovery. Those who exhibited high emotional intelligence looked inside themselves.

You have choices – choose life – you can't control what others do but you can control how you react.

That is EQ. That IS the wisdom of the ages.

Form Positive Habits

When we repeat conscious actions they are eventually turned into subconscious habits.

Referring back to our discussion on parts of the

brain and their specific functions, the basal ganglia part of the brain takes on the task of converting conscious acts into reliable unthinking habits.

Advances in scan technology are opening avenues into learning that were unheard of just a few years ago. Thanks to modern scans observers know that brain activity increases rapidly and significantly when you begin to develop a new skill.

Those skills are quickly converted from conscious activities, in large part, into habitual patterns. It becomes a habit (hopefully, a good habit) and gets turned over to your subconscious mind. Once that conversion is made the brain stops growing. It reaches a stopping point and then begins to regress.

This is why you must constantly hit the brain with new challenges, pushing limits and stimulating new growth. That is also why you must make positive choices as to what you will allow into your subconscious mind. This is especially true of repetitive actions and thoughts. They WILL become habitual, and you want those habits to support your needs and wants, not to thwart them.

Fill Your Subconscious With Positive Emotions

Let's look at several emotions that need to be emphasized, cultivated and nurtured on the path to heightened emotional intelligence.

Forgiveness is critical to achieving clarity in your mind which makes space for the maturity of emotional intelligence. Don't become addicted to hurting. When you hold grudges and refuse to forgive, you are renting space in your head to someone else for free. To forgive is the highest form of love and one of the MOST important expressions of emotional intelligence.

Another emotion that is important in developing heightened emotional intelligence is the feeling of gratitude. When paired with love and forgiveness, gratitude forms the great triumvirate of emotional intelligence. When things aren't going well, when you are feeling lonely or experiencing despair, stop and express gratitude for what you DO have.

These thoughts, if genuine and expressed with strong emotion, will attract like thoughts and feelings. Soon you will find that this process will lead you out of the darkness and into the light.

Build a core feeling of gratitude so that it becomes a foundation of core belief within your subconscious mind. This will cause you to be solution oriented rather than problem oriented. Solutions will come to you because your subconscious mind is your ally, not your opponent.

Compassion is one more emotion that should be included in your emotional intelligence developmental program. Compassion needs to be embedded into your subconscious at every possible opportunity. Practice compassion, and do kind things for others. You will begin to see opportunities for acts of kindness everywhere. Participating in those opportunities will bring more of the same from others toward you.

You also want to have compassion for yourself. This is a critical part of enhancing your emotional intelligence. Forgive yourself. Don't be harsh in judging your own mistakes.

Accept the past is over and done. Move on. Grasp the present with all your power, and anticipate the future with a knowing assurance.

Courage is also essential to the aspiring student of emotional intelligence. It takes courage to reject the advice of others, especially those who care about you. It often takes even more courage to reject the advice of the voice on your shoulder.

Take baby steps at first. Practice developing courage. It will come in small ways at first. Eventually, it will envelop you in a wave of self-confidence, gratitude, love and heightened emotional intelligence.

Constantly Replace Bad Experiences

There is a little understood, and seldom used, power to change your life. The subconscious mind doesn't know the difference between a real event and one that is vividly imagined. Read that sentence again. Then stop and think about the power it gives you.

Imagine you hit a bad golf shot. You don't want that thought to linger and become a part of your subconscious store of memories. Simply, replay the shot in vivid detail in your mind with a better outcome. You can literally erase the old memory and replace it with a positive recollection. Play the "good" story over and over. It becomes reality.

This same process can be utilized regardless of the type of incident. Be aware of this truth. Use it. Be empowered by it.

Repeat What You Want to Master

Repetitions are an important key to developing the kind of relationship you want to have between your conscious and your subconscious mind.

"Muscle Memory" is an important concept in fitness training and all sorts of athletic activities. You repeat. Repeat. Repeat. You repeat the effort – whether it is free throws, throwing darts, executing a dive or hammering a tee shot.

The same principle needs to be followed with what you are seeking to implant firmly into your subconscious. Nerve cells that fire together, wire together. Again, you have the immense human power to control this process.

Use these 6 steps. You will experience the rewards of, not just heightened emotional intelligence, but also, of increased cognitive fitness.

Monitor your thoughts. Stop throughout the day and ask, "What am I thinking at this second?" Is it a productive thought? Is it moving you toward where you want to go? Could it be replaced with a better, more constructive thought? How much emotion are you putting into the thought?

These are all critical questions to ask.

Your subconscious IS hearing every one of your thoughts. Those that are part of a pattern are building bridges or barriers within your subconscious mind. Your mind is consciously working. You can't decide to think of "nothing." Even when you try NOT to think of something, thoughts of that object are exactly what will occupy your mind.

I truly believe that when you learn how to place yourself into a deep state of relaxation and command EXTREME mental focus, you will enable your conscious AND subconscious minds, to open a clear channel of communication with your HIGHER SELF.

While in this state of mind, your creative abilities will blossom, and you will experience the ultimate power of intuition.

This is what I mean by BEYOND EMOTIONAL INTELLIGENCE!

One More Thing

Your thoughts are EXTREMELY powerful, especially if they are POSITIVE.

What I'm about to tell you, is BEYOND the SECRET. The Secret is a fantastic book written by Rhonda Byrne and I highly recommend it.

When I originally began working on my memory, I made up thousands of flash cards to study while on my exercise bike, as we already know.

One of the lists that I made was a list of 100 of the top male celebrities during that time. From that list of celebrities, I associated a list of movies, then a list of cities, then a list of phobias, etc. Gradually I developed what I call my "Mental Matrix." For example, number "30" on my list was Jay Leno, the movie for number "30" was "Jaws" (Jay's chin). The phobia for number "30" was selachophobia, (fear of sharks), etc. etc.

Number "30" and Jay Leno has over 300 different things associated with it, and so do the 99 other celebrities in my Mental Matrix. Pretty cool!

What's even MORE unbelievable is, that I actually met, (IN PERSON) 88 of the 100 celebrities that I placed on the flash cards!

This is only ONE example of HUNDREDS that I've experienced since venturing into the wonders of the Human Mind! More will be revealed in my NEXT book, which will be called "Mental Matrix."

The only person you should try to be better than, is the person you were yesterday.

Chapter 11

Sports and Emotional Intelligence

"Never let the fear of striking out get in your way."
—*Babe Ruth*

Emotional Intelligence happens to be very important when it comes to sports. Controlling your emotions plays a huge role in every sport. Whether you're a college athlete or a professional athlete, gaining higher emotional intelligence will not only improve your performance, it will also better prepare you "mentally" for high pressure situations.

Michael Jordan is a great example. He had great CHARISMA. He definitely INSPIRED his teammates. He was an amazing THINKER and a very good PROBLEM SOLVER. He always managed the EMOTIONAL STATE of all the players around him. I'm sure that when you looked into Michael Jordan's eyes, he was probably able to READ you as well.

SIX major components of higher emotional intelligence!

You take all of his amazing abilities, his skills of higher emotional intelligence and the extreme passion for the game and it's no wonder that Michael Jordan became the greatest basketball player of all time, and continues to be successful after basketball.

Joe Montana is another great example of an athlete with high emotional intelligence. He was always "cool as a cucumber," and had the character and leadership of a champion years before he became a great quarterback in the NFL.

In Montana's final game for Notre Dame, he led his team in a come from behind victory at the 1979 Cotton Bowl against the University of Houston. Being down 34 to 12 mid way through the 4th quarter, Montana brought his team back to win the game despite sitting out almost half of the game because of chills and running a temperature. Joe Montana definitely showed he was a LEADER, and was able to handle a VERY HIGH pressure situation successfully.

Montana's most unique example of high emotional intelligence took place in Super Bowl XXIII.

The 49er's were trailing (16 to 13) with only 3:20 left in game. They had the ball on their own eight yard line, 92 yards from the goal line. Montana recalled that some of the guys seemed very tense, especially his offensive tackle Harris Barton. After accessing the excitement and anxiety of his players while in the huddle, Montana pointed in the stands and said "Look, isn't that John Candy."

That wasn't what the players expected to hear in the huddle of a very tensed Super Bowl drive, but it worked! It definitely broke the tension. Everyone relaxed, smiled, and focused on the job that they all had to do. Montana and the 49er's drove the ball down the field and ended up winning the Super Bowl. Joe Montana recognized the emotional state in his players and handled it very effectively.

Hall of Fame broadcaster Tim McCarver tells a great story about Willie Mays that illustrates emotional intelligence at work.

Willie Mays is one of THE all-time greats. He had a long and distinguished career ending up with 660 home runs, 1903 RBIs, 338 stolen bases, a batting average of .302 and a slugging percentage of .384.

He was not only a great player but was one of the most charismatic figures to ever take the field. Fans would come to the ballpark early just to get a glimpse of Willie and to see him take batting practice.

McCarver revealed that Mays took a different approach to batting practice than other players. He would widen his stance and would not stride into the pitch during batting practice. He would swing only with his upper body.

The Mays approach showed keen emotional intelligence. He knew that in the game he would be seeing most pitches coming in at over 90 mph. In batting practice though the pitchers were throwing at around 60 mph. By keeping his lower body STILL during batting practice, he was better prepared to use his whole body under game conditions when he saw much faster pitches.

Willie Mays FOCUSED. He used his preparation time in the best possible way to maximize his game time performance.

That is a classic example of the kind of awareness shown by a person exhibiting heightened emotional intelligence.

There have been numerous coaches who have demonstrated high emotional intelligence throughout their career as well.

Some of MY personal favorites have been Tony LaRussa, Vince Lombardi, Pat Summitt, Knute Rockne, Mike Krzyzewski and Bill Walsh. A whole book can be written, just on these six coaches alone. Each one of them had amazingly high emotional intelligence and very successful careers.

Having good Emotional Intelligence as a coach is important at ALL levels. Coaching at the Little League level is probably the most important of all. As a Little League coach, these much younger players rely on you much more, and it is very important to stay POSITIVE and emotionally stable, because your attitude and decisions can impact these kids all the way through high school and college.

I mention this because I remember watching a Little League game once where the coach came out to argue a call and punched the umpire in the face. The coach from the other team came over and a huge fight broke out. We're talking LITTLE LEAGUE BASEBALL here! Keeping your COOL, is a big part of emotional intelligence.

Another extremely helpful and very important component of sports and emotional intelligence is VISUALIZATION. This is much easier to demonstrate than it is to describe. Visualization is an intense mental focus or ability to picture the outcome in your mind, seconds before it happens. This is taking emotional intelligence to a whole new level, going WAY BEYOND!

I have talked to several athletes who have the ability to do this. It takes lots of practice and 100% positive belief and focus.

I have demonstrated this MANY times myself, with games like darts, horseshoes, bowling, card throwing, free throw shooting, putting a golf ball or almost any kind of game or sport that requires "aiming." It is almost magical, how it works!

My personal example of "Mind Power" or visualization, is when I broke the Guinness World record for throwing a playing card over 200 feet.

I will NEVER forget the experience. Right before I was about to throw the "record breaking" card, I noticed a statue that was really far away, definitely more than the record of 150 feet that I was shooting for. My sights were focused on that statue, then I visualized myself throwing the card and watching it soar through the air hitting the statue.

I did this several times in my head before actually throwing the card. The best way to describe it, was like seeing a slow motion video in my mind. Then when I threw the card for real, it actually travelled along the exact same course as I plotted in my mind, just seconds before, and it ended up hitting the statue! When they measured the distance, it was 201 feet!

So I know from experience, that this hidden, amazing, visualization ability, truly does EXIST. And I also believe that each of us have this ability locked within our minds. The key to unlocking it comes from EXTREME, MENTAL FOCUS and POSITIVE THOUGHT.

Everywhere I travel, athletes ask me if achieving higher emotional intelligence can improve their game.

I believe that EVERY SINGLE ATHLETE ON THIS PLANET can definitely improve their game with heightened emotional intelligence.

The slump that you are currently in, the losing streak that you are experiencing, your low self-esteem and the stress and anxiety that you now feel, are all TEMPORARY, and can change in an INSTANT.

I recently began teaching cognitive fitness techniques to improve memory, focus attention, optimize health, control pain, and maximize all aspects of performance. These are ALL important components of enhanced emotional intelligence. Jim Karol's Cogmental Training has been used to help college and professional athletes, business leaders, and military veterans.

Cogmental Training

Cogmental Athletic Training will help a young, healthy athlete ENHANCE performance and achieve full potential. Cogmental Training ALSO helps experienced athletes with chronic pain, self-esteem, confidence, and memory issues. The program provides athletes guidance and inspiration to develop cognitive and behavioral regimens that will help them achieve their goals, prevent injuries, and improve overall mental and physical health.

Cogmental training focuses on Cognitive Enhancement and Higher Emotional Intelligence.

Proven Benefits Include:
    Overcoming Obstacles
    Enhance Visualization
    Improve Memory
    Increase Motivation
    Boosting Confidence
    Optimizing MENTAL Fitness
    Ability to READ People

Whether you have a healthy brain or a unique challenge, Jim Karol's Cogmental Training will help to develop Brain Excellence, which will lead to a more productive and POSITIVE life.

Poker and EQ

*"No one is skilled enough to win without LUCK, and no
one is lucky enough to win without SKILL." —Jim Karol*

This is a book about emotional intelligence and brain
wellness. This chapter, is dedicated to the role that poker
has played in enhancing my emotional intelligence.

This chapter is ALSO about the other side of that
equation – which is, how emotional intelligence makes
you a better poker player.

Let's pick up where we left off in the chapter on
neurotransmitters. We talked about neurotransmitters
and emotional intelligence in a general light including
IQ versus EQ.

Let's transition now and see how this all applies to
playing poker.

First of all, P= EQ². Meaning that Poker *can possibly
double* your emotional intelligence, making it much

stronger. Just playing Texas Hold 'em poker on a regular basis, will have a huge impact on the development of your emotional intelligence.

What's cool about being a part of the Texas Hold 'em world is that the game has become one of the world's most popular past times. A lot of people may not have noticed, but over 100 million people throughout the world play poker on a regular basis. Think about that, 100 million people playing poker on a regular basis, including 60 million in the United States alone. What a target audience for any business!

That being said, playing poker and emotional intelligence, in my opinion, DEFINITELY go hand in hand, just like so many other things in this book.

I perform as a mentalist and I consult people on memory training, cognitive fitness and emotional intelligence, but I also happen to be a long time poker player.

I have worked with some of the most successful people in the world on how to increase their EQ. My clients have included CEOs, athletes, actors, trial attorneys, teachers, military people, and others looking to form a closer connection. They have all gained confidence and enriched their lives immeasurably by making the study and application of emotional intelligence and brain wellness an important part of their lives.

Some people know me only as a magician. Some only know me as a consultant to people studying emotional intelligence and cognitive fitness. Others know me as a mentalist or memory expert. I've also consulted with several top magicians, including a former winner on America's Got Talent. In truth, I am all of those things and proud to say, I love what I do!

But all of the things I have done, and am doing, come together in the world of poker.

Some of the most rewarding and revealing work I've done in the area of cognitive fitness and emotional intelligence has come while studying the performances of renowned poker players.

Poker makes you stay alert and focus. It reduces stress and increases cognitive function. The connection between poker and emotional intelligence is undeniable.

This fact isn't just coming from me. This isn't just the Jim Karol theory. Science backs what was originally theory and assumptions.

Research done at McGill University in Canada concluded that stress hormones dropped significantly during poker tournaments. The levels decreased as much as 20% as the players progressed in the games. This outcome is because of the intense focus required during a poker game which helps to eliminate a lot of thoughts and negative worries. You don't have a chance to be thinking negative thoughts because you're so focused. Focus is a neglected part of the process, and is a positive attribute to apply to everything that you do.

Poker improves the major cognitive functions of the brain. While playing poker you're constantly thinking. You're constantly learning. You're constantly adapting strategies during the game, checking out details and trying to read people around you. That constant focus is excellent exercise for the brain.

Harvard professor Charles Nesson confirms the fact that poker teaches valuable skills. He actually used poker in his classes to teach students about decision making.

His goal wasn't to create better poker players. It was to create better investors and risk managers and to help all his students make better life decisions.

One of the skills you learn in poker is the ability to make well-reasoned bets. This helps you identify, evaluate, select or eliminate poor investment options in life. A second skill is being able to recognize your opponents' strategy and story without revealing your own. That is the essence of emotional intelligence.

You put those two things together and you have an amazing poker player. You put those two things together and you're going to have an amazing lawyer. You're going to have an amazing businessman, a great coach, athlete, spouse, engineer, parent, leader or anyone else trying to manage the experiences of their life.

That is the essence of emotional intelligence.

In an article written by Prof. James McManus, who taught a course on the literature of poker in Chicago, he claims that poker primed the minds and careers of some of histories most influential figures.

Are you ready for this? Even Bill Gates may have had his career sparked by poker during his brief time at Harvard in the mid-70s. According to Prof. McManus, Microsoft CEO Steve Ballmer once claimed that Microsoft's early business plan was basically an extension of the all night poker games Bill and he used to play back at Harvard.

In addition, Bill Gates was once quoted as saying that in poker a player collects different pieces of information such as who is betting, what cards are showing, what this guy's pattern of betting and blocking is and crunches all that data together to devise a plan for his own hand.

Gates also indicated that his poker strategizing experience proved to be helpful when he got into business.

Bill Gate's close friend, Warren Buffet is a poker player too.

Both Bill Gates and Warren Buffett are also known to be great Bridge players, another fantastic game that builds great emotional intelligence. Bridge and poker are both great "brain fitness" games as well!

These brilliant minds are not using the term emotional intelligence, but that is, clearly, what it sounds like they are describing.

I was fortunate enough to play against a lot of professional poker players, primarily in the course of doing charity work. Even when charity was involved, believe me, these guys don't ever want to lose. Trust me, they all have a lot of pride. I learned a lot from them.

I once found myself pitted against Howard Lederer, known as the Professor, for his studious approach to the game of poker. He was seated to my immediate left. I tried to bluff him. He saw right through me. I tried again about 20 minutes later. He read me correctly once again!

Then, I had pocket Kings and another King came on the flop. I had three kings and I made the SAME EXACT bet that I did the other two times. The Professor immediately read me and folded.

He exuded HIGH emotional intelligence. He is one of the best players I have ever observed and is THE best I've ever seen when it comes to applying high emotional intelligence to poker.

I've also watched him from home on TV, and observed a few of his performances. He is a true champion, but he is not alone in his use of emotional intelligence in the poker world.

Someone who gives him a run for his money is Annie Duke, who happens to be his sister. When I watched Annie play it is obvious that she has memorized every possible scenario. She is so articulate. She is a tremendous example of someone who plays poker, first and foremost, with her BRAIN!

In poker, no one is skilled enough to win without luck, and no one is lucky enough to win without skill.

Using emotional intelligence as a skill will greatly improve your odds of being a winner. Confidence is a critical part of having strong emotional intelligence.

The best way to improve and build your confidence in poker is to know the odds or probability of the outcome, given any situation which might arise. If you are serious about poker you need to know the odds involved in the situations described on the following pages of this chapter.

Poker Odds

How to Count Your Outs:

- Before you can begin to learn how to calculate poker odds, you should first learn how to count your "OUTS."

- An "OUT" is a card which will make your hand.

- For example, if you are holding two hearts and the flop gives you two more hearts, then there will be nine hearts (outs) remaining in the deck to give you a flush.

- Remember there are thirteen cards in each suit, so all you have to do is subtract four from thirteen! 13 − 4 = 9.

- Counting "OUTS" is a very simple process. Just

count the number of "unseen" cards that will improve your hand.

- If you have two pair after the flop, you would have a total of "4" OUTS, to get a full house or better!

The Four/Two Count:

- A very simple method of calculating poker odds is the 4/2 count!

- Simply multiply your outs by "4" after the flop. This will give you the percentage of your chances of reaching your goal by the "river."

- After seeing the "turn", you would only multiply your outs by "2" because your chances would decrease with only one card left to be shown.

- If a player goes all-in after the flop, and you call, you're guaranteed to see both the "turn" and "river" cards.

- If you have nine outs then all you have to do is multiply (9 x 4) to get (36), or 36%!

Odds for Hold'em

- Here are a few helpful odds that you should know when playing Hold'em.

When you are dealt two face down cards in Hold'em the probabilities of being dealt:

Pocket Aces (220 to 1)

Any pocket pair (16 to 1)

Ace/King (82 to 1)

Ace/King (suited) (330 to 1)

AA or KK (110 to 1)

Any two "suited" cards (3.3 to 1) AA, KK or AK (46 to 1)

Chances of taking a pocket pair to the river and making "trips" or better: (4.2 to 1)

Chances of taking two "suited" cards to the river and making a flush: (15 to 1)

Probability of Making the Following on the Flop:

Trips from any pocket pair:

(8.3 to 1).. or about 11%

Full house from any pocket

  pair: (136 to 1) 0.74%

Four of a kind from any pocket

  pair: (407 to 1) 0.25%

Flush from Two "suited"

  cards: (118 to 1) 0.85%

Probability of 3 Card Flop Having:

Three of a kind (424 to 1)............................ 0.25%

One Pair (5 to 1)... 17%

Three suited cards (18 to 1)............................. 5%

Rainbow flop, no suited cards (1.5 to 1) 40%

Probability of Hitting Flop to River

Full house or better with Trips (3 to 1) 33%

Full house or better from Two pair (5 to 1) ... 17%

Flush from Four "flush" cards (3 to 1) 35%

Flush from Three "flush" cards (23 to 1) 4%

Straight from an Open Ended
draw (2.2 to 1) 32%

Drawing an Inside straight (5 to 1)........... 17%

My Best Poker Hands

1. Ace – Ace

   The best Hold'em hand you can get! Pocket aces will win more than any other hand.
   - 31% against 8 players
   - 55% against 4 players
   - 85% head to head

2. King – King

   This is the 2nd best Hold'em hand, but is still incredibly strong!
   - 29% against 8 players
   - 50% against 4 players
   - 82% head to head

3. Queen – Queen
   - 25% against 8 players
   - 45% against 4 players
   - 80% head to head

4. Ace – King (suited)
   - 23% against 8 players
   - 40% against 4 players
   - 70% head to head
5. Ace – King (off suit)
   - 20% against 8 players
   - 35% against 4 players
   - 67% head to head
6. Jack – Jack
   - 20% against 8 players
   - 40% againts 4 players
   - 75% head to head
7. 10 – 10
   - 19% against 8 players
   - 36% against 4 players
   - 72% head to head
8. Ace – Queen (suited)
   - 19% against 8 players
   - 33% against 4 players
   - 66% head to head
9. King – Queen (suited)
   - 19% against 8 players
   - 33% against 4 players
   - 64% head to head
10. Ace – Queen
    - 18% against 8 players

– 31% against 4 players
– 63% head to head

If you can memorize some of this information, you will be able to access it whenever necessary. It will also be great exercise for the brain.

Knowing the odds is an essential part of playing winning poker.

Here are 10 important tips:

1. Don't be afraid to fold. Most of your great players fold more than half the time before seeing the flop!

2. Notice whether the people you are playing against, play loose or tight, or if they play aggressive or not.

3. If you are dealt pocket aces, try to get as many players out of the hand as possible! Less players, better the odds!!!

4. You can always learn from BETTER players.

5. You need to always FOCUS and stay extremely sharp when playing.

6. When you are tired or fatigued, take a break! If not, you will make more mistakes.

7. PATIENCE, PATIENCE, PATIENCE. You will last much longer!!!

8. Always take mental notes on your opponents. This is where a good memory comes in handy.

9. Never, EVER drink alcohol while playing poker.
10. NEVER get angry. Always keep your cool, no matter what!

Good Luck!

Summary

To sum everything up, there are hundreds of websites out there talking about memory enhancement, brain exercise, mind wellness, mind games, and emotional intelligence.

So what makes me, Jim Karol, so different from the others?

Not only have I learned HOW to achieve higher Emotional Intelligence, Brain Wellness and transcend my memory, but –

I am EXPERIENCING IT!

I am LIVING IT!

I fully UNDERSTAND IT!

I have personally, totally reconstructed my OWN brain and my way of life, and it was driven by EXTREME PASSION.

It also came with some fringe benefits, like improving my health and putting me in the best shape of my life, both physically and mentally!

The human brain has extraordinary, PHENOM-ENAL, capabilities that exceed far beyond what science has demonstrated! The brain is hundreds of times more powerful than all the biggest and most advanced SUPERCOMPUTERS on earth!

The BRAIN is a mini universe. There are billions and billions of NEURONS in the brain, just as there are billions and billions of STARS in the universe! We are only just beginning to explore BOTH!

I plan to continue exploring the UNLIMITED capabilities of the brain till the day I die!

"PASSION separates the BEST from the good ones."
—Jim Karol

If YOU make the RIGHT choices, get plenty of rest, stay physically and mentally Fit, surround yourself with good, POSITIVE people, eat the RIGHT foods, maintain a POSITIVE attitude and keep the Faith, not only will you achieve HIGHER emotional intelligence, you may just add another 10 to 15 HEALTHY years onto your life!

Appendix A

Understanding the terms and activities of the brain will help you take the steps necessary to move forward in your quest to achieve heightened emotional intelligence.

The brain also controls our thought, speech, and movement of our limbs. It controls the functions of the organs within our body. Our brain responds to stressful situations by regulating our heart, blood pressure and breathing rate. Understanding how the brain functions will be an immense aid in your quest for heightened emotional intelligence.

Our brain is encased and protected by "eight" fused cranial bones of the skull. At the base of the skull are numerous holes called "foramina." All of the arteries, veins and nerves from our brain, exit the skull through these "foramina". The BIG hole in the base of the skull is called the "foramen magnum." This is where the spinal cord exits.

The brain itself is composed of three major parts: Cerebrum, Cerebellum and Brain Stem.

The Cerebrum

The cerebrum is the largest part of the brain and is composed of a right and a left hemisphere, each divided into FOUR lobes. It is responsible for our speech, intelligence, emotion, reasoning and much more. The surface of the cerebrum is called the "cortex." The cortex is made up of "billions" of neurons and has a wrinkly, folded appearance that is called a "gyrus." The folding of the cortex, increases the brain's surface area allowing more neurons to fit inside the skull, enabling higher cognitive functions.

The Cerebellum

The cerebellum is located at the base of the brain, just above the brain stem. The cerebellum receives information from the sensory systems and the spinal cord, as well as numerous other parts of the brain. The cerebellum coordinates the voluntary movements like our posture, speech and coordination. It is also involved with learning motor behaviors. Almost half of the total neurons of the brain, are located in the cerebellum.

The Brainstem

The brainstem includes the midbrain, pons, and medulla, and acts as a relay center to the brain. The brainstem is involved with the body's automatic functions such as breathing, heart rate and body temperature and sleep cycles.

These major parts have multiple subdivisions which work together and allow us to perform the daily functions of our lives:

The Pons

The pons connects the cerebrum and the cerebellum and transfers sensory information throughout the brain. The pons also plays a key role in REM sleep and dreaming.

Medulla Oblongata

The medulla carries out the very important, crucial tasks of regulating our breathing and blood pressure. It also helps transfer neural messages between the brain and the spinal cord.

Right Brain/Left Brain

The brain is divided into the right and left hemispheres. The corpus callosum connects the two hemispheres, allowing messages to be transferred between the two hemispheres. Each hemisphere controls the opposite side of the body. The left hemisphere controls speech, comprehension, writing and math abilities. The right hemisphere controls creative abilities, like music and art!

Lobes of the Brain

The cerebral hemispheres of the brain are divided into four lobes. Frontal lobe, temporal lobe, parietal lobe and occipital lobe. The relationships between the lobes of the brain are very complex, and they all work in conjunction with each other.

Frontal Lobe

The frontal lobe is involved with things like emotion, personality, problem solving, intelligence and self-awareness. It is also involved with speaking and writing. The frontal lobe also regulates sexual urges!

Parietal Lobe

The parietal lobe is involved with the reception of all the sensory information from the body. The parietal lobe also interprets language, spatial and visual perception and more.

Occipital Lobe

The occipital lobe is the brains VISUAL processing center. The visual information exits the occipital lobe, and travels along the "VENTRAL" stream and the "DORSAL" stream. The ventral stream sends signals to the temporal lobe for memory and identification.

The dorsal stream sends signals to the parietal lobe for spatial location, reaching and grasping.

Temporal Lobe

The temporal lobe is involved with MEMORY, hearing and understanding language. The hippocampus is located in the temporal lobe.

The Limbic System

The Limbic system is a group of complex, subcortical structures of the brain, primarily responsible for our emotional life and higher mental functions, such as learning and memory.

Amygdala

The amygdala is responsible for the memory and response of emotions, especially fear.

Hippocampus

The hippocampus is important in forming new memories and also connects emotions and senses to memories. The hippocampus sends out memories to different parts of the brain, then retrieves the memories when needed.

Thalamus

The thalamus acts like a "relay station" for the information that circulates through the cortex. It also plays a role in memory, attention and pain sensation.

Fornix

The fornix is a band of nerve fibers that connect the hippocampus to the hypothalamus.

Hypothalamus

The hypothalamus functions as the thermostat of our body. The hypothalamus regulates our blood pressure and our body temperature, and also plays a part in controlling emotions, hunger and thirst.

Olfactory Cortex

The main role of the olfactory cortex is to identify odors.

Pituitary Gland

The pituitary gland helps promote bone and muscle growth. The pituitary gland also produces various internal secretions.

Pineal Gland

The pineal gland helps regulate the body's internal clock and circadian rhythms. It is also sometimes known as the third eye.

Basil Ganglia

The basal ganglia are a group of structures found deep in the sub cortical region of the brain. The basal ganglia are involved in the coordination of movement.

Meninges

The brain and spinal cord are covered and protected by three layers of tissue called "meninges." The three layers are called:

The Dura mater

The Arachnoid mater

The Pia mater

Cerebrospinal Fluid

Cerebrospinal fluid flows within and around the brain and spinal cord to help protect it from injury.

Blood Supply

Blood is carried to the brain by the "internal carotid arteries" and the "vertebral arteries." The brain's anterior circulation is fed by the internal carotid arteries.

Appendix B

Here is a list of some of the 12 digit barcode numbers that I learned while riding on my exercise.

There are 350 on this list, and I will soon complete my list of 10,000! Memorizing these 12 digit barcodes is my ULTIMATE brain exercise!

Barcode Numbers 1 to 350

001	056675242213	002	485331855652
003	093318855314	004	852943922913
005	393815206546	006	388998531359
007	352792954785	008	392293908154
009	893153180943	010	254166253116
011	310041354454	012	292235925856
013	255418454931	014	053814198190
015	053381995218	016	058408125201
017	184524119089	018	414454529058
019	055659396581	020	852580454985

021	544953186854	022	281469009354
023	393815205841	024	013149385295
025	952259058901	026	905254052589
027	292231881535	028	329405190355
029	013195381438	030	015254521590
031	913152201319	032	393815201319
033	385253819538	034	126139459012
035	419094856631	036	493521931754
037	152943590458	038	281353922992
039	141391442589	040	093122541221
041	755875325545	042	312175549470
043	391535589358	044	359255949659
045	053352550545	046	695835285941
047	951435445853	048	412944138524
049	853184905842	050	857996892294
051	818899546584	052	151418552598
053	893818475857	054	454652319894
055	358714685531	056	853150584954
057	388990568583	058	905251190941
059	388990914921	060	718599459591
061	905254951712	062	294495952183
063	610893190531	064	292253859012
065	015358861413	066	294352117844
067	412942500583	068	354145289544
069	819952238535	070	129353556580
071	852580854658	072	611245331445

073	493145205458	074	152942135478
075	715409401814	076	812185714281
077	129951081689	078	212192358385
079	388995454452	080	391505954018
081	292275242587	082	412941871500
083	414151855412	084	058475543145
085	412943566586	086	254909225899
087	535439295461	088	566559251845
089	852580453455	090	058859689475
091	819829321178	092	292258592259
093	054905318092	094	140549521445
095	318854251005	096	754581313141
097	140854585619	098	058445456631
099	013595182054	100	097583554978
101	018199936181	102	149312851956
103	650450530925	104	389451206985
105	213105085610	106	819885183590
107	250812351654	108	944565445435
109	498054143947	110	183175445416
111	755439228140	112	325955435140
113	090149329081	114	658859071368
115	399995493659	116	785195014999
117	058394105811	118	785329498147
119	853512545658	120	755465221911
121	252582589229	122	697803212935
123	085410181205	124	165375543549

125	853158199910	126	658899215225
127	785902190589	128	498058188553
129	118105194389	130	013905497809
131	981600161400	132	613556635253
133	213109543892	134	085754610858
135	819431421881	136	354198493181
137	695245648513	138	495818425214
139	085310582559	140	291829181221
141	210314755879	142	058853171985
143	119094653589	144	612669309544
145	354942213121	146	912947689210
147	081529593132	148	509582911443
149	901831892127	150	754539080853
151	944914105459	152	085310894853
153	685005353147	154	695385497589
155	981398141854	156	085853198170
157	085455881405	158	135893147816
159	129549252549	160	165225139114
161	144589957565	162	089625418354
163	901808515756	164	852547556085
165	039905861413	166	253552453949
167	085545839904	168	085396184565
169	721491058292	170	312257150193
171	085909476909	172	085819025845
173	488518945831	174	655025595785
175	192229221131	176	453514085658

177	197554199075	178	056714385109
179	935405613531	180	817947212201
181	938944258929	182	938513187540
183	221592850858	184	085629409054
185	685453545452	186	355008561854
187	411595681661	188	281258518054
189	414359390835	190	785909619400
191	319122143129	192	812253554951
193	013119941325	194	658852545615
195	254495144325	196	916583141190
197	992543556085	198	385352105613
199	621450560851	200	085785543925
201	452131854525	202	654495221491
203	453058955085	204	755879110214
205	354453093108	206	319913819500
207	318521441441	208	951083185294
209	453813698985	210	298794918938
211	453558112214	212	458083185294
213	885459921446	214	258354035406
215	154013156814	216	054459955419
217	589535213219	218	251999141210
219	944914194491	220	399999996690
221	922945999689	222	121213135407
223	319451171901	224	399951890566
225	181149192900	226	393897142149
227	625894101221	228	054191190940

229	953145935945	230	399354994314
231	312965849191	232	394459501919
233	585754912530	234	114919056511
235	359029879491	236	452141318954
237	452819112943	238	352581454542
239	458084115012	240	951084115016
241	354014185254	242	319894705452
243	941852599500	244	355394738555
245	101891202115	246	512185315121
247	353354935914	248	189654168554
249	121911014511	250	813199854521
251	452584521318	252	818899218765
253	085405445305	254	102140175587
255	818065843544	256	259054319913
257	144165299318	258	352132919510
259	354358445381	260	893835442987
261	122145453558	262	812597845808
263	685294543588	264	354065295825
265	681416580154	266	419829225054
267	352132195895	268	210558517525
269	944914165299	270	013195439999
271	968947695249	272	354075458512
273	117190131945	274	056658954390
275	290025853118	276	214994739389
277	012218199556	278	119094054190
279	459359459953	280	314995439935

281	913813540531	282	919406112394
283	912535857540	284	056511114919
285	381825905435	286	318954390545
287	294352445281	288	454258352581
289	299318314580	290	695885951084
291	852541354014	292	525369131989
293	259959418500	294	385554453553
295	912021153905	296	512185313905
297	914016545335	298	685549418965
299	014511121911	300	854521218131
301	998152058191	302	652144318913
303	314141500131	304	693212358181
305	681435618993	306	359018931914
307	785414190755	308	154514198529
309	354935354935	310	167814990141
311	454318135654	312	856122935608
313	290811491292	314	819096580566
315	085218131941	316	014999101499
317	119089129544	318	814718521416
319	658129310556	320	128194519528
321	456121108314	322	935454905318
323	058414183143	324	939065821442
325	819991359353	326	944914534528
327	354752911214	328	531145871905
329	389412590947	330	215929540914
331	016140515591	332	352532192575

333	389259140917	334	901258535126
335	218819431413	336	493181711314
337	385318561229	338	252145425981
339	958914131931	340	122149109814
341	755879109229	342	312181214131
343	358533581210	344	497584913553
345	214721459841	346	295041381459
347	313254916453	348	958291144354
349	212718919568	350	689296694593

Appendix C

On December 22nd, 1990, Jim Karol Correctly Predicted the Lottery!

The REAL Story of the "222" Dream

It happened on the night of November 2, 1990. I remember going to bed early that night, because I had to travel to a show early the next morning.

During the night I had the most realistic dream that I ever had in my life. I dreamed that the phone rang, and when I answered it, a man's voice said, "Jim, you were right! The daily number on December 22nd really was 2-2-2!"

I woke up immediately after the dream and wrote the number and date on a pad beside my bed. It's a good thing I wrote it down, because in the morning when I woke up, I didn't remember the dream.

After breakfast, I was getting ready for my show and my wife came up to me and said "what does 2-2-2

December 22 mean?" As soon as she said that, the whole dream came to back to me.

That evening, after my show I told everyone in the audience to play 2-2-2 on the Pennsylvania Daily Number December 22nd.

The next night, and after ALL of the shows that I had through December, I told the audiences the same thing – play 2-2-2 December 22nd, and you will win!

I made this prediction at more than 35 Holiday shows, not knowing if the people really took me seriously or not. I had numerous dreams that came true in the past, but this one felt really special.

Psychic predicts winning lottery numbers — & costs state $12 million!

Thousands hit jackpot by playing his 'dream combo'

Jim Karol had a psychic dream about the winning daily numbers in Pennsylvania's lottery, so he gave the numbers to thousands of people who bet them — and it cost the state nearly $12 million!

A whopping 39,863 players had the unusual winning combination of 2-2-2, said lottery commission spokesman Mark Schreiber. "This resulted in a payout of $13,883,700 — and the state brought in only $2,112,444 in sales."

The usual daily payout is only about $1.1 million, according to Schreiber.

Karol, a comic/magician, says that in the weeks following his dream he told people at 41 of his shows to play 2-2-2 on December 22 of last year — and word spread like wildfire. Those who heeded his advice won an average of $348 each!

"It's impossible to determine how many people followed Jim Karol's winning advice, but it must have been considerable," said Schreiber.

"We were just fortunate that his prediction didn't get on TV before the numbers were drawn, otherwise we could have been hit for as much as $45 million!"

Among the lucky winners was Kenneth A. Hantz, former chief of the Lehigh Township Volunteer Fire Company, who disclosed:

"About 50 of our fire fighters and auxiliary members are richer by a total of $372,000 because we took advantage of Jim Karol's startlingly accurate prediction."

Karol, who lives in North Catasauqua, Pa., said his eerie forecast came to him as he was sleeping last November 2.

"I dreamed that I picked up the phone and a man's voice said, 'Jim, you were right! The daily number on December 22 really was 2-2-2!'"

Karol told The ENQUIRER, "The dream was so real that I felt compelled to share it with my audiences. I'd never done that before.

HE'S 2-2-2 MUCH: Jim Karol with one of the lucky lottery tickets.

I told more than 8,000 people at my shows."

Sure enough, the numbers came up!

The lottery brings Pennsylvania an average profit of nearly $1 million per day — so losing $12 million in one day came as a complete shock and surprise!

The payout was so huge because in Pennsylvania you can bet 50 cents or $1, with a guaranteed payout of $500 for each $1 bet if you pick the numbers in the right sequence.

Karol, who bills himself as the "Psychic Madman," admitted he doesn't really consider himself psychic. But he doesn't have any other explanation for the mysterious way he picked the right numbers.

Ironically, Karol wasn't among the nearly 40,000 winners — because he didn't buy a ticket himself!

"I forgot," he explained.

— *RICHARD BAKER*

They won $72,000

Jim Karol's premonition paid off for these happy members of Lehigh Township Volunteer Fire Company.

Finally the big day – December 22nd – arrived. I was getting ready for a show that night and was in such a rush, that I never got to play the number for myself.

After my show, I rushed home, anxious to find out what the winning daily numbers were. As I walked by my answering machine, I noticed that the light was blinking, so I stopped to listen to my messages first, and had 67 messages in my mailbox. I began to listen to them and when I got to the 3rd message, it said, "Jim, you were right! The Daily number was 2-2-2." It was the SAME voice as in the dream, but now I recognized it as the fire chief from a local fire department where I had just performed for their holiday party. The chief wanted to let me know that the group of firefighters had won a total of $72,000 from my prediction.

The other messages were from other people who had won from hearing my prediction as well.

I had calls from newspapers and TV news programs all across the country. The AP jumped all over the story because it happened right before Christmas.

A lottery spokesman later said "the average daily number payout was usually about $1.1 million, but because of the 2-2-2 prediction, over $13 million dollars had been won." He also said "we were fortunate this prediction didn't get on TV before the numbers were drawn, we could have been hit for as much as $45 million!"

Despite the lottery directors' concerns, I felt great that those people had won extra money for the holidays.

About a week later, I was contacted by several tabloids and ended up giving the story to one of them. The following week, over 23 million people were reading about my 2-2-2 dream. I received hundreds of letters and phone calls from people asking me for lotto numbers in their states. For the next several weeks, I couldn't go anywhere in Allentown without being approached by people asking, "What numbers should I play?"

Is it possible that the collective minds of the thousands of people that heard my prediction, all wishing for 2-2-2-, actually made it happen! WHO KNOWS?

Appendix D

11 original vocabulary words which I created and their meanings:

Cogfit – A person that masters cognitive fitness.

Cogmental – The most paramount achievement in cognition and emotional intelligence.

Cogmentalist – A mentalist that uses cognition and memory in his presentation.

Cogmentalism – Study of mentalism, memory, cognition and emotional intelligence

Memelection – The ability to skillfully combine memory, reason and knowledge.

Memitate – To review memorized information in quiet thought.

Memitation – The act of reviewing memorized information in quiet thought

Mental Matrix – A very complex pattern of numerous, memorized lists that syncretize successfully with each other.

Mindwiz – A person with extraordinary mental abilities.

Nimjim – A person that successfully defeats Jim in his infamous game of logic. (Impossible)

Oculoreaction – The non-verbal clues that the EYES throw off.

Appendix E

Cranial Nerves

#	Name
1.	Olfactory nerve
2.	Optic nerve
3.	Oculomotor nerve
4.	Trochlear nerve
5.	Trigeminal nerve
6.	Abducens nerve
7.	Facial nerve
8.	Vestibulocochlear nerve
9.	Glossopharyngeal nerve
10.	Vagus nerve
11.	Spinal Accessory nerve
12.	Hypoglossal nerve

Appendix F

I have Karol has memorized the names of every one of these movies. If you happen to meet me on the street, in an airport or at a performance, test me. Give me a number and I'll give you the name of the movie. Or name the movie and I will tell you what number it is on the list.

Notice that there are 366 movies on the list! Each movie also represents a date on the calendar.

Example:

1)   January 1st, is the first day of the year

100) April 10th, is the 100th day of the year

150) May 30th, is the 150th day of the year

200) July 19th, is the 200th day of the year

250) September 7th, is the 250th day of the year

300) October 27th, is the 300th day of the year

If you happen to be born on February 29th, the number 366 is your movie and number!

Movies 001 to 366

1. Jurassic Park
2. Animal House
3. Ace Ventura Pet Detective
4. Mrs. Doubtfire
5. Back to the Future
6. Rush Hour
7. Lethal Weapon
8. Independence Day
9. Dirty Dancing
10. Armageddon
11. Good Will Hunting
12. Close Encounters
13. Titanic
14. Forrest Gump
15. Mission Impossible
16. Grease
17. Terminator
18. Gremlins
19. Home Alone
20. Good Fellas
21. Beverly Hills Cop
22. Fight Club
23. The Natural
24. A Few Good Men
25. Rocky
26. Ferris Bueller's Day Off
27. Ghost Busters
28. Dirty Harry
29. Karate Kid
30. Jaws
31. Shaft
32. Face Off
33. Vacation
34. The Godfather
35. Rain Man
36. Con Air
37. Field of Dreams
38. Die Hard
39. The Waterboy
40. Liar, Liar
41. Batman
42. Jerry Maguire
43. Austin Powers
44. Pulp Fiction
45. Men in Black
46. Saving Private Ryan
47. True Lies
48. E.T.
49. Star Wars
50. Gone With the Wind

51. Indiana Jones
52. The Matrix
53. Pretty Woman
54. Psycho
55. Shawshank Redemption
56. The Rock
57. The Deer Hunter
58. American Graffiti
59. Alien
60. Apollo 13
61. Under Siege
62. XXX
63. Star Trek
64. Revenge of the Nerds
65. Twister
66. Be Cool
67. The Exorcist
68. The Wizard of Oz
69. Gladiator
70. Cable Guy
71. The Sting
72. The Hustler
73. 48 Hours
74. Footloose
75. Kill Bill
76. No Country for Old Men
77. As Good As It Gets
78. Top Gun
79. Scent of a Woman
80. Raging Bull
81. Schindler's List
82. Scream
83. Blues Brothers
84. The Flintstones
85. Phenomenon
86. Meet the Parents
87. Dukes of Hazzard
88. Braveheart
89. Dances with Wolves
90. Ghost
91. Casablanca
92. Halloween
93. Jackass Number Two
94. Zorro
95. Bonnie and Clyde
96. Superman
97. Silence of the Lambs
98. Chocolate Factory
99. Planet of the Apes
100. The Green Mile
101. The Lost World

102. Carrie
103. Dumb and Dumber
104. Good Morning Vietnam
105. The American President
106. Earthquake
107. Signs
108. I am Legend
109. The Dirty Dozen
110. Ben Hur
111. The Departed
112. King Kong
113. Poseidon Adventure
114. Toy Story
115. War of the Worlds
116. Hairspray
117. Jingle all the Way
118. Taxi Driver
119. Casino
120. The Fan
121. Coming to America
122. Snatch
123. Basketball Diaries
124. One Flew Over the Cuckoo's Nest
125. Rambo
126. The 40 year old Virgin
127. Scrooged
128. The Good, the Bad & the Ugly
129. Enter the Dragon
130. Shrek
131. Snakes on a Plane
132. Night of the Living Dead
133. Christmas Vacation
134. Scarface
135. A Beautiful Mind
136. Knowing
137. The Untouchables
138. The Sixth Sense
139. The Longest Yard
140. Wild Hogs
141. The Dark Knight
142. Men of Honor
143. Wayne's World
144. White Men Can't Jump
145. Men in Black 2
146. Tomorrow Never Dies
147. The Pink Panther

148. Kalifornia
149. Private Parts
150. Dazed and Confused
151. The Fugitive
152. Day the Earth Stood Still
153. American Beauty
154. Remember the Titans
155. Oh God
156. Iron Man
157. Batman Returns
158. The Wrestler
159. Mars Attacks
160. Aladdin
161. 12 Angry Men
162. The Fast and the Furious
163. Star Trek: Generations
164. Blazing Saddles
165. Pay it Forward
166. Fred Claus
167. The Pianist
168. Conan the Barbarian
169. 3:10 to Yuma
170. School of Rock
171. The Way We Were
172. The Color of Money
173. Another 48 Hours
174. Hollow Man
175. Kill Bill 2
176. The Hulk
177. Ali
178. Airplane
179. Batman and Robin
180. Rebel Without a Cause
181. Easy Rider
182. Saw
183. Trading Places
184. The Babe
185. The Prestige
186. Something About Mary
187. Dodge Ball
188. Prince of Darkness
189. Midnight Cowboy
190. Poltergeist
191. Rushmore
192. Citizen Kane
193. Jackass

194. "V" For Vendetta
195. Heaven Can Wait
196. The Quick and the Dead
197. The Elephant Man
198. Pirates of the Caribbean
199. To Sir With Love
200. Splendor in the Grass
201. Goldfinger
202. American Pie
203. Bruce Almighty
204. The Talented Mr. Ripley
205. Back to the Future 2
206. Jailhouse Rock
207. Maverick
208. Wild Wild West
209. Dirty Rotten Scoundrels
210. Hollywoodland
211. The Bourne Identity
212. Godzilla
213. Gangs of New York
214. A League of Their Own
215. Interview with the Vampire
216. Get Shorty
217. Predator
218. Deck the Halls
219. American Gangster
220. A Bronx Tale
221. Beverly Hills Cop 2
222. Seven
223. Hoop Dreams
224. The Shining
225. Rocky 2
226. Gigi
227. Caddyshack
228. High Plains Drifter
229. Chinatown
230. Shrek 2
231. The Negotiator
232. Dawn of the Dead
233. Vegas Vacation
234. Serpico
235. The Graduate
236. Leaving Las Vegas
237. Eight Men Out
238. The Whole Nine Yards
239. Mr. Deeds

240. The Santa Clause
241. Ocean's Eleven
242. Million Dollar Baby
243. Wayne's World 2
244. Major League
245. Transformers
246. Patton
247. Inglorious Bastards
248. The X Files
249. Howard's End
250. Clueless
251. Raiders of the Lost Ark
252. The Replacements
253. Life is Beautiful
254. Malcom X
255. Driving Miss Daisy
256. Tooth Fairy
257. Dr. Jekyll and Mr. Hyde
258. Lord of the Rings
259. Mission to Mars
260. Shane
261. Twelve Monkeys
262. Speed
263. Star Trek 2: Wrath of Khan
264. Analyze This
265. Suicide Kings
266. Wedding Crashers
267. The Piano
268. Escape to Witch Mountain
269. Cinderella Man
270. Alice in Wonderland
271. Out of Africa
272. Cool Hand Luke
273. Cape Fear
274. My Dog Skip
275. Vertigo
276. Grumpy Old Men
277. It's a Wonderful Life
278. Blue Sky
279. Spider-man
280. Dangerous
281. Ghandi
282. Saw 2
283. Dragnet
284. Arachnophobia
285. David Copperfield
286. Mary Poppins
287. Starsky & Hutch

288. The English Patient
289. Sherlock Holmes
290. Ghost Rider
291. Look Who's Talking
292. Robo Cop
293. Spartacus
294. The Addams Family
295. Shampoo
296. Unforgiven
297. Hannibal
298. Donnie Brasco
299. The Lion King
300. Happy Gilmore
301. Golden Eye
302. American Pie 2
303. The Mask
304. The Thing
305. Back to the Future 3
306. Rush Hour 2
307. Lethal weapon 4
308. Bad Boys
309. The Breakfast Club
310. The Sum of all Fears
311. The Adjustment Bureau
312. Fathoms
313. Inception
314. Cast Away
315. The Firm
316. Michael
317. Kindergarten Cop
318. Twins
319. My Cousin Vinny
320. On the Waterfront
321. Lawrence of Arabia
322. Troy
323. Space Jam
324. Mutiny on the Bounty
325. Rocky 3
326. It Happened One Night
327. Groundhog Day
328. All Quiet on the Western Front
329. Bloodsport
330. Up
331. Amadeus
332. The African Queen
333. The Three Musketeers
334. To Kill a Mockingbird
335. Meet the Fockers

336. City of Angels
337. Angels in the Outfield
338. Boys Town
339. Mr Deeds Goes to Town
340. The Apartment
341. Hotel Rwanda
342. Slumdog Millionaire
343. Weekend at Bernie's
344. Blade Runner
345. The Maltese Falcon
346. Peyton Place
347. Our Man Flint
348. Invasion of the Body Snatchers
349. The King and I
350. Clue
351. Air Force One
352. The Matrix Reloaded
353. Beauty and the Beast
354. Black Swan
355. Apocalypse Now
356. The Scorpion King
357. Walking Tall
358. Fargo
359. Red Planet
360. 2001: A Space Odyssey
361. High Noon
362. Rear Window
363. X-Men
364. Oscar
365. Midnight Run
366. Total Recall

Books for Further Reading

General Editor: Professor Peter Abrahams, How the Brain Works. New York: Sterling Publishing, 2015

James Allen, As a Man Thinketh. New York: Penguin Group, 2006

Daniel Goleman, Focus – The Hidden Driver of Excellence. New York: Harpercollins, 2013

Richard J. Davidson and Sharon Begley, The Emotional Life of Your Brain: How its Unique Patterns Affect the Way You Think, Feel and Live – and How You Can Change Them. New York: Plume, 2012

Michael Posner and Mary Rothbart, Educating the Human Brain. Washington, D.C: American Psychological Association, 2006

Gary Small, M.D., The Memory Bible – An Innovative Strategy for Keeping Your Brain Young. New York: Hachette Books, 2002

Dean Hodgkin, B.Sc., Physiology and Fitness. Virginia: The Teaching Company, 2012

Harold S. Kushner, When Bad Things Happen to Good People. New York: Avon Books, 1981

Dan Hurley, Smarter – The New Science of Building Brain Power. New York: Penguin Group, 2013

Bruce H. Lipton, Ph.D., The Biology of Belief – Unleashing the Power of Consciousness, Matter & Miracles. Hay House, 2008

Dr. David Walton, Emotional Intelligence – A Practical Guide. New York: MJF Books, 2012

Yeung, Emotional Intelligence: The New Rules. Cyan Books, 2009

Michio Kaku, The Future of the Mind – The Scientific Quest to Understand, Enhance and Empower the Mind. New York: Doubleday, 2014

Miriam Boleyn-Fitzgerald, Pictures of the Mind: What the New Neuroscience Tells us About Who We Are. New Jersey: Harper Perennial, 2011

Rob DeSalle and Ian Tattersall, The Brain: Big Bangs, Behaviors and Beliefs. Connecticut: Yale University Press, 2012

Ray Kurzweil, How to Create A Mind: The Secret of Human Thought Revealed. New York: Viking Books, 2012

Daniel Tammet, Born on a Blue Day: Inside the Extraordinary Mind of an Artistic Savant. New York: Free Press, 2006

David Eagleman, Incognito: The Secret Lives of the Brain. New York: Pantheon Books, 2011

Marcus Buckingham and Donald O. Clifton, Now, Discover Your Strengths. New York: Cardoza Publishing, 2003

Eric Kandel, In Search of Memory: The Emergence of a New Science of Mind. New York: W.W Norton, 2007

Stephen L. Macknik and Susana Martinez-Conde, Sleights of Mind: What the Neuroscience of Magic Reveals About our Everyday Deceptions. New York: Henry Holt, 2010

S. Blakeslee and M. Blakeslee, The Body Has a Mind of Its Own. New York: Random House, 2007

CPSIA information can be obtained
at www.ICGtesting.com
Printed in the USA
LVOW02s1116070216
474069LV00007B/32/P